CONCILIUM

Religion in the Eighties

CONCILIUM

Editorial Directors

Concilium 170 (10/1983): Retrospect and Prospect

TWENTY YEARS OF *CONCILIUM*—RETROSPECT AND PROSPECT

Edited by
Paul Brand,
Edward Schillebeeckx
and
Anton Weiler

English Language Editor
Marcus Lefébure

T. & T. CLARK LTD
Edinburgh

THE SEABURY PRESS
New York

December 1983
T. & T. Clark Ltd, 36 George Street, Edinburgh EH2 2LQ
ISBN: 0 567 30050 1

The Seabury Press, 815 Second Avenue, New York, NY 10017
ISBN: 0 8164 2450 0

Library of Congress Catalog Card No.: 82 062763

Printed in Scotland by William Blackwood & Sons Ltd, Edinburgh

Concilium: Monthly except July and August. ISSN: 0010-5236.
Subscriptions 1983: UK and Rest of the World £27·50, postage and handling included (new subscribers £25·00); USA and Canada, all applications for subscriptions and enquiries about *Concilium* should be addressed to The Seabury Press, 815 Second Avenue, New York, NY 10017, USA.

CONTENTS

Editorial

Nineteen Years of *Concilium*

IN 1984, *Concilium* will begin its twentieth year. This seemed a good opportunity for the editorial directors to look back critically at the past and at the same time to look forward at the future. Before doing this, however, it seemed sensible to give our readers some information about our way of working in this international journal, since quite an important and complicated part is played by both the 'collective' and the 'personal' aspects.

1. *CONCILIUM*'S WAY OF WORKING

The 'board of editorial directors', that is, all the editors-in-chief of the journal, some thirty-five theologians from different countries and continents, meet annually in plenary assembly together with the publishers of *Concilium* and decide on the themes for the coming year. Suggestions are then made in an initial 'brainstorming' as to how the themes ought to be developed. The ten themes for the year are then discussed in greater detail in three groups. After the annual meeting, advice is obtained in writing about these themes from the eleven 'advisory committees'. These are formed according to theological disciplines. Each of the sections has about thirty-five theologians, so that the total membership of the whole advisory committee is about 350.

An initial 'provisional', but quite detailed plan of each issue of *Concilium* in the year concerned is then made by the two directors responsible for that issue on the basis of the suggestions made at the annual meeting and by way of written consultation. This initial plan is then considered both by the editorial directors and the advisory committee. This is also done in writing. This may or may not result in changes of a fundamental or a secondary nature being made in the provisional plan. The two directors then act on their own authority and, on the basis of these new reactions and having taken into account all the suggestions that have been made to them, formulate the definitive plan for the issue. This is sent for information to the members of the board of editorial directors and the advisory council respectively. The two directors now have the task of looking for authors, partly on the basis of suggestions made to them. Each author is given the opportunity to inspect the definitive plan as a guideline for writing his article. The two editors-in-chief have to make sure that the articles for their issue are completed and they have to approve them when they come in. They do this with the help of the General

Secretariat in Nijmegen. In several cases, the two editors-in-chief live so far apart from each other that the practice has developed in several sectors for only one of them to assume ultimate responsibility for the issue in alternate years. ·

The time allowed between deciding on the theme at the annual meeting of the board of editorial directors and the appearance of the article and the intervening process usually operate perfectly. Sometimes, if the first author defaults, it is necessary to write to a second. Occasionally a third or even a fourth author has to be approached. It is very exceptional for an emergency measure to be taken because an author fails to produce his article because of illness or for some other reason. The authors are bound to work within the framework imposed on them by the collective decision of the board of editorial directors and by the plan formulated by the two directors on the one hand and the tendency to be followed in the issue as determined by the latter on the other. Otherwise, the authors are quite free to choose the way in which they want to write their articles.

It should be clear from this that the two directors have considerable influence, especially in their choice of authors and their editing of the final plan of the issue, but that they are also subject to the restriction imposed on them by the initial collective decision. In the early years of *Concilium*, the director had what amounted to an exclusive right to decide, but the board of editorial directors put an end to that in 1968-69, when changes were made in the management of the journal, making it more democratic.

Two years, then, elapse between deciding on the themes for all the issues in a given year and the appearance of those issues in print. *Concilium* is also an international journal in which the same articles appear in seven different language editions. This means that the journal cannot possibly be geared to publishing articles of urgent contemporary interest. It is therefore concerned with more profound problems of the kind that are, in any case, usually at the source of those urgent contemporary questions. It is in fact remarkable how often a theme that was planned two years before the appearance of the articles is of deep contemporary interest.

2. *CONCILIUM* 1984: A YEAR OF TRANSITION

In a concluding article in this issue, the *Concilium* Foundation gives its reasons for changing the structure of the journal by adding two new sections, one on feminist theology and the other on Third World theology. The decision was taken, however, as early as 1982 to reduce the issues per year from 1984 onwards from ten to six. This will mean a lower subscription rate in these years of economic recession, but this is not the main reason for producing fewer issues per year. For several years now, we have been asked to produce fewer than ten issues, because many readers find a thousand pages of *Concilium* a year—and there are approximately as many pages as that in ten issues of the present format—too many. In addition to its normal function as a theological journal, however, *Concilium* is also used by many of its readers as a kind of reference work for ten different theological disciplines. Because of this, the committee of management has always been reluctant to suggest a reduction. Having finally decided on this, we hve done everything possible to retain the advantages of the earlier structure by devoting one issue to each theological discipline not every year, but every two years. It will therefore be obvious that twelve sections have to replace the original ten and that there will consequently be twelve advisory committees in future. In the space of two years, all the disciplines will be presented once and *Concilium* will, despite the concentration on themes, preserve its broad theological spectrum. Because of the timing of a year's issues two years before their appearance, 1984 has to be a year of transition, in which directors of various disciplines will be responsible for the six themes chosen for that year.

Concilium will, however, continue to be a theological journal with a pastoral and a political and hermeneutical slant. The themes chosen for the twentieth year of its publication will in themselves give readers a good idea of the direction that it intends to follow in the future: (1) Various forms of theology and our joint responsibility: Babel or Pentecost? (2) Liberation as a challenge to Christian ethics; (3) Sexuality in religion and society; (4) Handing on faith to future generations; (5) Judaism as a radical question put to Christian theology; (6) Third World theology.

3. THE LAST ISSUE: NO. 170

NINETEEN YEARS OF CONCILIUM

In this last issue of the nineteenth year of the publication of *Concilium*, the editors-in-chief not only look back critically at the issues that have appeared during their term of office, but also look forward at the future of the journal. They do this from the particular vantage-point of their own theological discipline. This procedure could be described as their examination of conscience. They consider what they have done in the past and ask themselves if they were really proceeding in the right direction. They also ask themselves whether certain emphases should be changed or whether they should be reinforced. They then go on to suggest certain directions that might be followed in the future in their own disciplines.

What is quite clear from this look at the past is that theologians are much more modest now than they used to be. They teach less and listen more. They listen to what is going on in the world and among believers. They are also conscious of what is going on in 'orthodox' circles and in 'anti-official' circles and they are mindful of the whole history of human suffering. They discover blind spots in comtemporary history and tendencies that they believe should be strengthened. They are aware of all this because of the light shed by the great Jewish and Christian history of experience and interpretation and the ups and downs of the Christian community and those who are their pastoral guides. In this sense, then, *Concilium* tries to justify the hope on which we all base our lives. *Concilium* works within the paradigm of a God who is concerned for man and wants to liberate him and who comes to us in the person of Jesus of Nazareth, confessed as the Christ. Within that paradigm, it is urged by its own self-critical attitude and by the challenge offered by others to continue to carry out its constructive and sometimes possibly subversive task in constantly changing situations. It does not claim to be the only journal or publication performing such a function in a Church that is now seen to be polycentric, but it does want its own distinctive voice to be heard.

'What is truth?' This question can be asked by a hungry and exploited worker in the Third World. It can also be asked by an unemployed man in the West trying to make both ends meet or by a woman living in a male society and a male Church. It is then quite a different question from that asked, with the same words, by the prosperous Westerner or by Pilate when confronted by Jesus. Part of the task of *Concilium* in the future is to ask precisely that question, confronted by cultural contexts in society that are both externally and internally divided. It can, moreover, only be answered after a patient search and a great deal of experimentation and on the basis of what theologians can learn from the grass-roots in the Church and the world.

We asked Odilo Metzler to try to discover to what extent *Concilium* has in the past given space to the various forms of Third World theology. Finally, we also asked two older theologians, Karl Rahner and Yves Congar, both of whom have worked as pioneers for *Concilium*, to give us their honest opinion of the journal. They hesitated, but eventually accepted our invitation and we would like to thank them for their wise and sympathetic criticism and promise to take it to heart.

The task of translating articles from their original languages into six other languages and various cultures can only be carried out by skilful translators who are able to find the right new equivalents for a constantly developing theology. We are particularly grateful to the men and women who serve the authors and readers of *Concilium* in this way.

Concilium is not a 'school of theology', but, despite all our mutual differences, we do aim to follow a common policy as human beings and as Christians, especially in those cases when Christian mankind is bruised or in some way undermined. Christian identity and human integrity are, however, not simply theoretical questions and for this reason a real attempt will be made in future issues of *Concilium* to make the dialectical tension between theory and praxis more clearly visible.

At the end of this issue, the four theologians of the *Concilium* Foundation provide a picture of the 'new face' of this journal from 1985 onwards, that is, after the year of transition in 1984.

PAUL BRAND
EDWARD SCHILLEBEECKX
ANTON WEILER

Gregory Baum

Sociology of Religion 1973-1983

THE PLANS for a new series of *Concilium* in 1970 included the creation of a new division called 'Sociology of Religion'. One issue a year was to be dedicated to the dialogue between theology and the social sciences. The mandate was not quite clear. The name, Sociology of Religion, suggested that the dominant approach would be social/scientific, in particular, sociological. When the first issue came out in 1973, some readers were surprised to find in it theological reflections and some sociological articles written from a faith perspective. It was necessary to explain in the editorial of the second issue (1974) that the section, 'Sociology of Religion', was dedicated to interdisciplinary studies. The editorial admitted that it was difficult to find an appropriate name for the section. 'It is difficult to categorise studies that bring together various disciplines examining the phenomenon of religion—theology, sociology, psychology, etc.—for they fit into none of the recognised subdivisions of theology nor can they be identified with social science or any of its branches.' Was it confusing, then, to call this division 'sociology of religion'? The editorial explained: 'To refer to the issues of *Concilium* devoted to this multidisciplinary approach as sociology of religion would be misleading were it not for the fact that these issues belong to a theological journal.' The issues of 'Sociology of Religion' are addressed first of all to a theological readership.

Methodologically much remains unclear. The editors opted for a pluralism of approaches. Because of the multiplicity of viewpoints, the individual issues of 'Sociology of Religion' do not usually offer a coherent perspective. They do not establish important conclusions. There are exceptions to this which I shall mention in a moment. The individual issues are valuable because they cover a great deal of ground: they deal with topics of great importance to the Church and its pastoral policies, topics that for some reason or other have not been dealt with in other divisions. It is useful to recall the titles: *The Persistence of Religion* (1973), *The Church as Institution* (1974), *Intellectuals in the Church* (1975), *Women in the Church* (1976)—the last two never appeared in English—*Ethnicity* (1977), *Communications in the Church* (1978), *The Family in Crisis or in Transition?* (1979), *Work and Religion* (1980), *Neo-Conservatism: Social and Religious Phenomenon* (1981) and *The Church and Racism* (1982).

Clear conclusions emerged only from three issues, *The Persistence of Religion*, *Women in the Church* and *The Church and Racism*. The sociological orientation affirmed in *The Persistence of Religion* I shall examine in some detail further on. Both *Women in the Church* and *The Church and Racism* established the heritage of oppression in the Christian tradition itself as well as the Christian efforts at the present

1

time, thanks to the emancipatory struggles of the subjugated, supported by all who love justice, to overcome domination and unfold the full meaning of the Gospel for the Church.

1. ALL OF THEOLOGY IN DIALOGUE

There is no discernible development in the ten issues of 'Sociology of Religion'. Methodological pluralism and the lack of coherence among the approaches used by sociologists and theologians did not allow such an evolution. The one important development to be recorded is that over the last ten years the dialogue of theology and the social sciences has come to be recognised in all the branches of theology and for that reason is being carried on today in all the sections of *Concilium*. This is obviously true for 'Moral Theology' and 'Practical Theology' which deal with Christian action in society and therefore with matters that are political in the wide sense of the term. But today all branches of theology have entered into dialogue with sociology—on several levels.

There is first of all the principle known in biblical studies under the name of *Sitz im Leben*, which asserts that the meaning of a religious utterance or a theological proposition cannot be fully understood unless its social location has been clarified. This is a principle belonging to the sociology of knowledge. If it is useful for the study of biblical passages, it is equally applicable to the study of religious utterances and theological statements made in the Church throughout its history. Theologians have come to recognise that doctrinal statements and theological developments of past and present cannot be fully grasped unless their relation to the social base has been clarified. To grasp the contextual nature of theology, dialogue with sociology is indispensable.

Secondly, theologians have learnt from sociology to recognise the cultural power of ideology. Church teaching, theological developments, liturgical pattern and forms of spirituality must be examined in regard to the extent to which they protect the ecclesiastical institution and legitimise the power interests of the dominant classes. From dialogue with sociology theologians have learnt that the proclamation of the Gospel and its theological explorations have an effect on culture and society and hence exercise a political function, 'political' here being used in the wide sense. Theologians can no longer shrug their shoulders in regard to the historical consequences of their theories and explanations. Theologians are beginning to recognise that the truth question in Christian faith is not settled in abstract, conceptual terms but in terms that include the impact of religion on people's lives. Here again dialogue with the sociology of culture is inevitable.

Finally, it is worth mentioning that various branches of theology have entered into dialogue with the appropriate social science: thus liturgical theology is in conversation with the anthropology and sociology of worship, ecclesiology with the sociology of organisation, and personal ethics with psychology.

A glance through the recent issues of *Concilium* reveals that this development has in fact taken place. If we examine, for instance, the 1981 and 1982 issues on 'Dogmatic Theology' we notice immediately the ongoing dialogue with sociology. In the issue entitled *God as Father?* we find two articles that reveal at a glance the critical social science reference, 'God the Father in the Fatherless Society', and 'The Murder of the Father and God the Father in the Work of Freud'. In the issue called *Jesus, Son of God?* we find two articles whose titles suggest sociological reflection, 'A Crucified People's Faith in the Son of God', and 'Son of God and Sons of God: The Social Relevance of the Christological Titles'. These are samples. If we look at the recent issues of any of the other divisions of *Concilium* we find evidence of the same dialogue with sociology.

Someone may wish to argue that because of the evolution of contemporary theology it is no longer useful to have a special division of *Concilium* that concentrates on the multidisciplinary approach. I would not go quite so far. It seems to me that the division 'Sociology of Religion' still has the task of moving into new fields of inquiry, to raise issues that theology has often left unattended, and to provide articles following a variety of perspectives so that theologians are able to choose that particular approach in social science with which they want to engage in dialogue.

2. PLURALISM AND CONFLICT

As we read through the last ten issues of 'Sociology of Religion' we are struck by the pluralism of methodologies. There is no coherence in the approaches adopted by editors and authors. Such a pluralism may be inevitable, particularly at the beginning of interdisciplinary research. Pluralism may even be something worth protecting. It is nonetheless useful to clarify some of the differences in methodology. I wish to mention two conflicting approaches in particular.

The first difference of approach is found not only in the articles published, but even in the editorial planning. Some issues of 'Sociology of Religion', for instance *Ethnicity* and *The Family in Crisis or Transition?*, divide the material into two distinct parts, the first written by sociologists offering the readers the sociological analysis of the social reality, and the second written by theologians presenting the readers with theological reflection on the state of affairs. This organisation of the material suggests a special division of labour in the interdisciplinary research: the sociologists clarify the facts, and theologians reflect on these facts in the light of divine revelation. There are some good reasons for adopting such a division of labour. It protects the independence and integrity of the disciplines: sociologists remain sociologists and theologians theologians. It corresponds to a certain common-sense expectation, widely spread in the public, that sociology is a 'hard' science using scientific method to establish its conclusions, while theology at best belongs to the 'soft' sciences that rely on interpretation.

The greater number of the articles published in 'Sociology of Religion' do not follow this division of labour. Why not? Because value-perspective cannot be separated from sociological research that easily. The social sciences are not natural sciences: they study human beings, and for this reason they inevitably operate out of a value perspective. They approach the social reality from a certain angle. Even if one argues with Max Weber that formal reasoning and scientific tools employed in the social sciences are value-neutral, universal, independent of culture and social location, and in this sense 'objective', one must admit with Weber that individual sociologists inevitably operate out of a value-perspective of their choice. Weber defends a moment of voluntarism in the social sciences. The values brought by sociologists to their research affect their manner of 'reading' the social reality: they affect the questions they ask, the conceptual tools they create for themselves, and the sensitivity with which they observe the social reality. The value-free nature of formal reasoning does not guarantee unanimity among sociologists.

Many sociologists go much further in their acknowledgment of the value-perspective operative in the social sciences. They claim that social science research is always carried by certain interests: according to some these interests are defined by the discipline itself, and according to others the interests arise from identification with certain social groups and social goals. In this perspective, sociology appears as a scientific exercise located in history with definable historical consequences. Since the value-perspective operative in the social sciences may be hidden, it is a special task to clarify the implicit values and examine them in a critical manner. Sociological research, therefore, is not devoid of ethical import. The separation of hard fact from soft values is an illusion. Social facts include meaning, and hence to clarify them is a hermeneutical task. And according to some sociologists, social facts are co-determined by a special activity of the human mind in carving them out of the unbroken continuum of the social reality.

There is a second difference of approach in the articles collected in the section, 'Sociology of Religion'. A good illustration is the contrast between two articles in the issue *Communication in the Church*, both dealing with opposition and tension in the Church. 'The Silent Majority' deals with conflicts in the American Church, and 'Currents of Opposition in the Spanish Church' deals with conflicts in the Church of Spain. The first article tries to understand the conflict in the Church in terms of the diverse religious aspirations of the people. The article, an exercise in the sociology of religion, looks upon the religious system as a cohesive historical entity that can be understood relying on factors intrinsic to it. The other article tries to understand the conflict in the Church by locating the religious community in the historical setting and studying the religious tensions in relation to the struggles and divisions taking place in society. What is assumed here is that the historical struggles of society are primary, and that whatever takes place on the cultural or religious level in society must be understood in relationship to the societal conflicts. A religious system cannot be understood out of itself. The first article deals with the religious conflicts in purely religious terms, while the second article tries to show how religious conflicts reveal their full meaning only if they are related to the social base on which they take place.

The second approach, while historically sounder, could lead sociologists into the temptation of overlooking the authenticity of religious conflicts and reduce them purely and simply to the rehearsing, on the religious level, of conflicts that have their real meaning in the profane order. In the history of sociology, reductionism has been a frequent phenomenon, especially in the area of religion. Sociologists have asserted, in accordance with one or another social theory, that religion was nothing but a cultural symptom reflecting a disorder in human society. It is therefore with good reason that theologians are cautious in regard to sociological approaches that have a built-in tendency to reductionism. Still, the sociological approach mentioned above, which refuses to understand religious experience in separation from the social reality in which it is grounded, need not be reductionist at all.

The section, 'Sociology of Religion', has been methodologically pluralistic. The two conflictual approaches mentioned above have been used in all the issues; and no attempt has been made to clarify the differences and to argue for their resolution. While this methodological pluralism has a positive function, the lack of methodological consistency has tended to make the individual issues somewhat incoherent: no clear conclusions flowed from the investigations. The exceptions to this rule were mentioned in a previous paragraph.

What this brief discussion reveals is that when theologians engage in dialogue with sociology or the social sciences in general they find themselves confronted by diverse trends in these sciences. Which one of these trends will they choose as their dialogue partner? The choice may not be arbitrary. Not all sociological approaches are equally appropriate. Theologians are not surprised by this methodological pluralism because they realise that there are different approaches in their own discipline.

It can be argued that theologians will look for a social science approach that has a certain 'affinity' with the theological approach they have adopted.[1] 'Affinity' is here the key word. Theologians who concentrate on the transformation of individuals through the coming of God's grace, who focus on persons, are likely to detect an affinity with a sociology of religion, such as Max Weber's, which also concentrates on religious persons, the charismatic founder and his followers. Tradition, for Max Weber, comes about through the institutionalisation of the founder's personal charisma. The vitality of a religion depends on the presence of gifted individuals, the *virtuosi*. Theologians who concentrate on the organic mystery of the Church, on God's gifts creating community, and who understand Christians as generated by these gifts, will detect a certain affinity with a sociology that sees society in organic terms, in other words with some form of functionalism, which understands persons in terms of the socialisation process through which they have been constituted. If theologians, on the other hand, stress above all God's Word as judgment on sin and as promise for new life, they are likely to detect an affinity with some form of conflict sociology, which recognises as the most visible feature of society its contradictions, its structural imbalances, its oppressive character. Conflict sociology tends to see the struggle to resolve these contradictions as the dynamic element of religion.

What I am proposing is that interdisciplinary research engaging theology and the social sciences must have an inner coherence. There is nothing arbitrary about the choice of approaches in any of the disciplines. If there is no congruence, no affinity, between the approaches adopted in the different disciplines, the interdisciplinary project will lead to confusion and eventually break down. The disciplines will not take their partner in the dialogue seriously, they will not learn from one another, they will remain extrinsic to one another, and instead of co-operating in the project they will become competitors.

From these brief remarks I wish to conclude that it may be useful for theologians, and hence for the readers of *Concilium*, if the section, 'Sociology of Religion' carried forward interdisciplinary research with special attention to the question of methodology. Contemporary theologians must be acquainted not only with the methodological questions of their own discipline but also with the methodological problems of the disciplines with which they are in dialogue. I do not propose that the 'Sociology of Religion' section abandon its pluralistic face: what I suggest is that more attention be given to methodology in the interdisciplinary treatment of current issues affecting the Church's life.

3. THE PERSISTENCE OF RELIGION

At the end of this article I must turn to a controversial topic, in which the 'Sociology of Religion' section has taken sides. The most provocative issue was the first one, *The Persistence of Religion*. In it the great majority of the articles offered evidence against what is often called 'the theory of secularisation'. According to this theory, defended by many sociologists from the nineteenth century on, the advance of modernity leads to the waning of religion. According to this theory, there is a conflict between traditional religious consciousness and modern consciousness defined by rational society. To the extent that people are drawn into science, technology and democracy they lose the sense of religion and perceive themselves in wholly secular terms. In countries such as France and England, empirical research has confirmed the theory of secularisation.

The first issue of 'Sociology of Religion' gathered evidence against this theory. The empirical evidence drawn from a variety of cultures and societies suggests that there is no fixed sociological law relating religion and modernisation. In each part of the world it is necessary to make an independent inquiry into the impact of modernisation on religion.

This first issue was severely criticised. Some European critics suggested that the issue was apologetic: it defended a theological anthropology. Others suggested that it reflected an American experience and contained elements of ideology. They referred to Bellah's work on the civil religion of America, which shows the place of religion in

American cultural consciousness.[2] To be a good American one has to be either religious or at least sympathetic to religion. This trend exists in a strongly ideological form. Religion then becomes a legitimation of American power in the world. In a Cold War perspective, the world appears divided between two empires, the good empire of believers and the bad empire of atheists. At the present time, there are Christians not only among the sects but even among the major denominations who argue that Christian faith demands wholehearted support for the American cause in the world.

It is important to remember, however, that the ideological use of Christianity does not exhaust the Christian heritage of America. Recent historical research has established that the millenarian movement known as the Great Awakening, which swept through the British colonies in the eighteenth century, created symbols of rupture with the existing order, an urgent sense of expectancy and a collective will for independence, and as such laid the cultural foundation for the American Revolution. Religion was part of America's revolutionary experience.[3]

When in the 1830s Alexis de Tocqueville visited the United States he was amazed by the presence of religion among the people. He argued that in this vast country marked by great horizontal and vertical mobility, religion fulfilled important social functions.[4] It provided people with a sense of community and it corrected their individualism. Since religious convictions enabled people to resist the power of public opinion, Tocqueville thought that religion in America protected people's freedom. When Max Weber visited the United States at the beginning of the twentieth century, he confirmed Tocqueville's observations: in fact, he found additional sociological reasons why religion was so universally practised in that country.[5] While since then the educated classes in America have become much more secular, religion continues to be honoured and plays an important role.

It is important to remember that religion in America assumes a variety of socio-political orientations. There is conservative religion; there is a lot of religion supporting right-wing politics; there is liberal religion, and there is the religion of the left. Working class struggles and protest movements in America (and English Canada) have usually been supported by an appropriate religious current. While at present we witness an influential sectarian religious movement, the Moral Majority, which supports the policies of the Reagan Administration, there is also a significant religious movement in the major denominations, based on the religious yearning for social justice. This movement exists in the Catholic Church where it has a special history. The recent draft statement of the United States bishops on nuclear disarmament and the 1983 New Year statement of the Canadian bishops on unemployment and the economic crisis are expressions of this radical trend. The presence of religion in American culture cannot be reduced to ideology: it is related to profound social experiences in the history of the country. (The same must be said for countries and cultures where the entry into modernity has led to rapid secularisation: here too the waning of religion is related to important social experiences.)

Even though in many countries indifference to religion is widely spread and almost assumes a dimension of universality, the section 'Sociology of Religion' has resisted any theory that affirms a necessary link between modernisation and the decline of religion. At one time the American experience was the great counter-argument against the theory of secularisation. Today other arguments have been added to this. There is the vulnerability of secularised societies to surrogate religions; there is the surprising success of the so-called new religions in Western society: and there is a return to religion, albeit in a new key, among Asian, African and Latin American nations struggling to enter into modernity in their own original way. The editors of 'Sociology of Religion' think they are justified in pursuing this perspective. In fact, the January 1983 issue is entitled *New Religious Movements*.

Notes

1. In the following typology of affinities I rely on W. Everett, T. Bachmeyer *Disciplines in Transformation* (Washingon, DC, 1979).

2. R. Bellah 'Civil Religion in America' *Religion in America* ed. W. G. McLoughlin (Boston 1966) pp. 3-23.

3. Alan Heimert *Religion and the American Mind* (Harvard 1966).

4. A. De Tocqueville *Democracy in America*, II, Book 1, ch. 5.

5. M. Weber 'The Protestant Sects and the Spirit of Capitalism' in *Max Weber* ed. Gerth and Mills (New York 1946).

David Power

People at Liturgy

THE CHANGES in liturgical text and celebration that were made possible by the decrees of the Second Vatican Council seemed to fulfil many of the aspirations of those who had been active in the preconciliar liturgical movement. At the same time, enacting these changes presented a considerable challenge to the Church, universal and local. The issues that *Concilium* has devoted to liturgy since its inception reflect the various questions that had to be faced as the nature of the challenge became more apparent.

1. REFORMS AND RETRIEVAL OF TRADITION

Three principles enunciated by the Vatican Council were uppermost in determining the first phase of the reform, as they were also uppermost in the studies presented to guide and explain it.[1] First of all, it was the aim to so order the rites that the active participation of the congregation would be encouraged to the greatest possible degree. Secondly, much was made of the need to restore the pristine structures and forms of Church worship, since these had been grossly obscured by the accretions of over a thousand years, under the influence of elements in piety and Church life that were not appreciative of the sacramental and symbolic, and accommodated sacramental practice to peoples who did not know the tongue in which liturgy was rendered. Thirdly, great care was taken to foster simplicity of language and clarity of signs, so that the faithful could readily understand the meaning of rites and ceremonies. In its early issues, *Concilium* participated in promoting this kind of development. Its aim was to make known and understood the biblical foundations of liturgy and the content and purpose of the conciliar norms, as well as to give appropriate historical information on such matters as the rites of initiation and funeral liturgies, which were in the process of reform.

2. THE SYMBOLIC AND COMMUNITY

One of the things that had dogged the development of the Roman liturgy through a thousand years was that it had been subjected to many external changes that would render it attractive to common piety, without ever undergoing the kind of internal restructuring that would assimilate and educate the prevalent forms and expressions of this piety. Popular devotion flourished alongside the liturgy, often accompanying it, but was never truly integrated into it. In the prayer books and missals with which the laity were furnished up to the time of the Council, there were often explanations of the parts of the mass that owed more to the allegories on the mass of ninth- and tenth-century commentators than to its early history or inner structure. Not a few schoolchildren were brought up in the fifties thinking that when the priest washed his hands at the lavabo he was re-enacting the gesture of Pilate during the trial of Jesus.

Even the Council did not seem to think much in terms of integration of piety and liturgy, contenting itself with the observation that popular devotions should be renewed in such a way that they could foster better participation in the liturgy.[2] The issue, however, of the relation between popular devotion and public worship had been raised in the decades immediately preceding the Council and there was considerable debate as to whether one could make a clear split between official prayer and the prayers of the church's faithful.[3] One oft-cited example was the true nature of the difference between a common recitation of the rosary and a common recitation of the divine office. The official ruling repeated in documents that themselves were intended to foster liturgical growth was that liturgy comprised all that was contained in the officially approved liturgical books.[4] This was but a canonical answer to a theological and pastoral question. It was in line with much that had happened in earlier centuries when prayers such as the rosary or the stations of the cross became the chief nourishment of the laity. The substitution of Paters and Aves for psalms had been a device whereby to give the laity ignorant of Latin a kind of marginal share in the liturgy. As popular piety was modelled on the piety of the mendicants, it was thought that the devout should be able to pray the office as they did. Failing that, they could adopt a suitable substitute. In effect, however, it needed to be asked then, as it still needed to be asked in 1965, whether the Church as a community of faithful could give proper expression to its participation in Christ's mystery in ways that were attuned both to tradition and to contemporary culture and popular needs.

When it became possible to think of the liturgy as an action of the community instead of as a priestly act attended by the laity, the implications of this question became more obvious. It involved in the first place the need to have a better grasp of how symbols and rites give expression to a sense of community and of how they transform experience and articulate the holy. The editors of *Concilium* shared this concern with fellow liturgists and invited the collaboration of pastors, scholars, artists and other participants in liturgy in investigating the factors involved.

There is a marked difference between the studies that represent this phase of enquiry and those that accompanied the first phase of postconciliar change. Then it was usually asked what liturgical symbols and texts mean, and what diversity of symbolic expression may be found in different liturgical traditions. Good liturgy was somewhat behaviouristically conceived as the communication of right thought and sentiment through the enactment of correct prayers and symbols. What later studies tackled was the perception that liturgy's growth is organic, as is true of all symbol systems. They employed more sophisticated means of investigating meaning, appealing to such tools as structuralism and to such sciences as sociology, anthropology and psychology. These studies show the way in which meaning is given in context, and that by reason of different terms of reference the same ritual can be diversely understood and appropriated by different people. The presumption of some unqualified meaning and effect, issuing from a sacramental institution and tradition, is severely challenged by such awareness.

3. INTERPRETATION WITHIN LITURGY

There are three kinds of meaning that one may distinguish in the actual celebration of liturgy. First of all, there is the meaning that the ritual has when it is taken as a text within a tradition, with a potential to be appropriated. There is, however, also the meaning that is given to the ritual by the participants when they employ it to refer to their own world of reference, one which may not be coterminous with the traditional sense of the ritual. This naturally affects the organic growth of the ritual and the ways in which it is passed on, to what moments of life it belongs, in what circumstances it is celebrated, and so on. One also has to make a further distinction, that between the meaning which may be given to the ritual by the official Church representative and that which is given by the other participants.

This can be illustrated by looking at the role of the presider in a liturgy. For many participants, especially on such occasions as weddings and infant baptism, since the presider is a priest he is in their world of reference the guarantor of divine blessings and of protection against evil. As the chief actor in an official ritual of the Church, he is on the other hand official representative and agent of a power that determines the reality of the Church as a social body. Many factors in the currently official law and ritual of the Roman Church identify this social power with the power of Christ. The symbols of blessing and divine power that belong within the Gospel's world of reference express a meaning that may be but poorly assimilated within the world of reference to which the other two meanings belong. Indeed, they may be partly stifled by the forms that have in the course of time been adopted to accommodate the official sense of the Church or popular perceptions.

Within this context, the concern with the pristine liturgy of the first years of the reform takes on a new perspective. The aim of such interest cannot be to restore this kind of celebration. Rather it is to find a point of reference and a criterion of judgment whereby to assess the ongoing organic growth of the Church's worship.

4. CRITICAL REFLECTION

These issues surfaced already in treating of such matters as the meaning given to the Scriptures in the course of celebration, the influences of popular piety on worship, the politics of liturgical change, or the structures of Christian initiation. A more self-conscious development of critical methodology can be seen in some of the articles that appear in the issues on the frequency of eucharistic celebration and on creativity in liturgical development. This critical phase of liturgical studies is sorely needed in order to overcome the gradual decline of good liturgical celebration in some places and in order to allow liturgy to be an integral part of new ecclesial developments through which Christian engagement in human existence is being newly expressed.

Religious sentiment and religious expression are highly ambiguous phenomena. The fact that they belong within the Christian populace or that they are sanctioned in liturgical publications is no guarantee against this ambiguity. Liturgical study has to learn from the methods and perceptions of critical hermeneutics and critical theory, if the apostolic tradition is to be given expression in new cultural situations. It is necessary to understand what has shaped liturgical development over the course of time, to recover and express what had been forgotten or suppressed, and to take account of the pluriformity of liturgical expression. It is common enough to speak now of the one faith and the many theologies. Similarly, one might speak of the one worship of God in which churches participate through a variety of liturgies. Since it is an international review, *Concilium* can only write of liturgy as multicultural.

There are three parts to the kind of critical reflection here proposed. First of all, elements of critical theory need to be evolved that are appropriate to the study of liturgy and that it make it possible to see the cultural and ideological factors that have influenced the shape of worship but are not identifiable with its core. Secondly, attention needs to be given to the connection that liturgy has with experience and praxis. Thirdly, more has to be said about acculturation, since the liturgical movement has scarcely begun to tackle the issues raised by the Vatican Council when it laid down the norms for the adaptation of liturgy to the temperament and traditions of peoples.[5]

5. CRITICAL THEORY AND LITURGY

Certain difficulties encountered in the course of liturgical renewal can only make those with a knowledge of history and of biblical symbolism suspicious. There is a sense that things ought to be other than they are. Though the new *Ordo Paenitentiae* enunciates the principle of the communal nature of the sacrament and gives texts for communal celebrations, one is hard put to find a congregation in which the community is the real locus of the experience of God's forgiveness. What has happened to penance and what is maintained in the new *Ordo* that prevent the retrieval of such an experience? The suspicion in face of this and other examples is that there are blocks in the life of the Church as a society and institution that hinder growth.

Critical theorists are well aware of how much symbolic interaction is at the centre of all social interaction and pursuit of common interest and values. They also point out, however, that symbolic interaction can actually reflect specific power systems and promote the ends of particular interest groups or secure the stability of society by establishing the dominance of a particular group of élite. What they then look for is the breakdown in symbolic interaction that prevents participation and interaction of subjects, giving rise instead to various forms of domination. Their interest is in a strategy that fosters the interaction between subjects in the pursuit of common values and common interest. To realise this they see the importance of restoring effective symbolic interaction.

A number of theologians have applied this kind of thinking to elements of Church institution, such as Church structures and dogma, as well as to the Church's involvement in emancipatory praxis within society.[6] Its application to liturgy would seem to touch the heart of Christian community, since this is the place of symbolic expression and interaction where the Church comes to be as a faith community. Liturgists will be interested in seeing what factors of Church life in the course of centuries prevented the liturgy from expressing a community in which there is neither Jew nor gentile, rich nor poor, male nor female. They will also want to ask what led to a symbolic expression which seemed to identify the kingdom of God with a system, and God's power with the clergy. The biblical images of hope that are emancipatory and that, if kept at the heart of liturgy would prevent this kind of identification, seem to have been ossified.

One of the things that this critical interest means for liturgy is that it will change the character of its memorial prayer, not of course by replacing Jesus Christ and his death, but in the way in which this mystery is remembered. No society that looks for emancipatory change will achieve it without taking the whole of its past into account. If it looks to the future because of the hope that is given in an originating event, it will not retrieve this without making sense in recollection of all that has happened in between. To the extent that it values its origins for the way in which it expressed the dignity and freedom of persons, it will be obliged to take mind of those who in betweeen have been disallowed a part in the life of the society or who have suffered domination and oppression.

Writers of political theology speak of the need for anamnetic solidarity of the oppressed.[7] When the Christian community looks to the future in the hope of God's reign, it must perforce remember in Jesus Christ all the suffering and oppressed of the past, all those for whom the Church has failed and still fails to take a prophetic stand or in whose oppression it has played a part.[8] It cannot do this without looking to its own liturgical structures, to the domination of clerical elements, to the absence of women in the ministry, and to the neglect of what is expressed in forms of popular piety.

As far as forms of liturgical prayer are concerned, more attention will have to be given to lament, where Old Testament paradigms may serve anew.[9] Recent studies on the origins of the eucharistic prayer include the *todah* as well as the *berakah* tradition.[10] While this is essentially a prayer of thanksgiving and supplication prompted by deeds remembered, it was shaped in part by lament and confession of sins. Looking to God's past wonders, the people of Israel also wanted to make sense in this remembrance of sufferings and infidelities. When calamity occurred, God had as it were to be named anew, even as the name revealed in the burning bush was recalled.

6. LITURGY AND PRAXIS

Such thoughts turn our attention to the link between liturgy and Church praxis, or to the way in which liturgy relates to experience. The experience here intended is twofold. On the one hand, liturgy carries the power of symbolic expression to transform all experience by the formulation of meaning, by making out of the world which surrounds us a world of significance. On the other hand, the liturgical community will have special interest in the particular experience of those whose lives and action and prayer can be diagnostic for the whole Church.

There are in the Church not only individuals but whole communities that are deeply in touch with suffering, with the humanity that is threatened by oppression and absurdity, and yet within that experience are in touch through faith with the memory of Jesus in his death and with the belief that God does not abandon those who are in agony. Out of such living experience, these persons find ways of Christian engagement, of shaping community, and of prayer that are in contrast with much that goes on in the rest of the Church. They can point to what is missing or at fault in the established ways. In other words, the Church can find itself revealed in the mirror of such groups because of their faith and engagement.[11]

Liturgical development in this critical phase has to attend to such contrast realities. There are many instances that could be quoted. In the United States of America, there are women's groups that convene for feminist liturgies in which that which has been long suppressed in the life of the Church is given voice. This is not just a claim to right, but in the very best sense of the word it is affirmative action done in faith. Eventually, one would hope for the integration of this experience into the full life of the Church. In a number of Third World countries, there are basic Christian communities in which people come to new ministerial structures and new kinds of prayer and symbolic action out of an experience of engagement in faith and hope with the poor and suffering. In places like the North of Ireland where populations are torn apart by religious differences, there are communities that are coming to an actual realisation of what it means to integrate in one worship Catholic and Protestant traditions.

7. INCULTURATION

In writing of liturgical adaptation, Anscar Chupungco distinguishes between cultural adaptation or acculturation and inculturation. Acculturation he describes as the process 'whereby cultural elements which are compatible with the Roman liturgy are incorporated into it either as substitutes or illustrations of euchological and ritual elements of the Roman rite'.[12] Inculturation he describes as the process 'whereby a pre-Christian rite is endowed with Christian meaning'.[13] That this twofold process continue to develop in liturgy is all the more necessary because it has much to do with the issue already raised of suppression in the tradition, of marginalisation of groups and of suffering. Many of the poor and oppressed continue to find their most meaningful religious expression in the non-liturgical adaptation of traditions that are older than the advent of Christianity to their soil. Since these express the peoples' needs more deeply they hold on to cultural traditions that have never been integrated into the Church or society, but tend to be ignored or despised. One also notices that those groups who live by the hope of Jesus Christ in the midst of human suffering are often the groups that are most alert to the values of the cultures that have been trodden upon. Although in the past *Concilium* has given some attention to acculturation and inculturation,[14] the matter requires more persistent investigation and thought, in a way that links it to Church praxis and experience.

8. FUTURE PROJECTS

The analysis of the liturgical development with which *Concilium* has tried to keep in touch in past issues carries within itself the seed of future projects. Historical studies will continue to be important. Every day research throws new light on historical questions. Paying attention to a diversity of forms and to the cultural aspects of past development allows us to see the ways in which the core Christian symbols and rites are at work and also the ways in which poor or ideological development can obscure or distort their meaning. We can introduce an element of dialectic into liturgical study which replaces the tendency to look for pure and univocal forms.

As the prayer of a people of faith, liturgy for its own development has to attend to non-liturgical prayer and to the prayer that is on the fringes of liturgy. Here it is that one sees how people strive to relate the memory of Jesus Christ to their lives, and from this we understand better what has to be integrated into worship. Not only do we find such prayer in the past, but we also find it in the present. Not only are there popular movements of devotion but there is also the prayer of those groups that because of their involvement in human suffering and the courage of their faith and hope in the God of Jesus Christ, furnish the rest of the Church with models of Christian engagement and with models of the prayer of remembrance.

Though one cannot foretell exactly what topics of liturgical interest will be taken up by *Concilium* in the future, what has been said here will have to influence the choice. What has been done in the past has brought us to a better grasp of where we now stand and to some vision of where it may be possible to go in the future.

Notes

1. Second Vatican Council *Constitution on the Sacred Liturgy*, Norms for the Reform of the Sacred Liturgy, nn. 21-46.

2. *Ibid*. n. 13.

3. For the story of this discussion see Salvatore Marsili 'La Liturgia, momento storico della salvezza' in *La Liturgia, Momento nella Storia della Salvezza* (Torino 1947) pp. 137-156.

4. Sacra Congregation Rituum *Instructio de musica sacra et sacra liturgia ad mentem Litterarum Encyclicarum Pii Papae XII 'Musicae Sacrae Disciplina' et 'Mediator Dei'* Caput I, 1, AAS 50 (1958) 632.

5. *Ibid*. nn. 37-40.

6. For an overview of how theologians relate to critical theory see Matthew Lamb *Solidarity With Victims. Toward a Theology of Social Transformation* (New York 1982) pp. 61-99.

7. Lamb, *ibid.*, pp. 7-12.

8. In his article in *Concilium* 172 (English 152) (1982) 'The Bread of the Eucharistic Celebration as a Sign of Justice in the Community' Enrique Dussel recalls the Church's compromise with the conquerors who oppressed the Indian peoples of Brazil. This is but one example from many in history.

9. Claus Westermann *Lob und Klage in den Psalmen* (Göttingen 1977).

10. Cesare Giraudo *La Struttura letteraria della preghiera eucaristica* (Rome 1981).

11. See Chapter IV in Edward Schillebeeckx *Ministry. Leadership in the Community of Jesus Christ* (New York 1981) (*Kerkelijk Ambt: Vorgangers in de Gemeente van Jezus Christus* Bloemendaal 1980).

12. Anscar Chupungco *Cultural Adaptation of the Liturgy* (New York 1982) p. 81.

13. *Ibid.*, p. 84. See Anscar Chupungco's articles in *Concilium*: 'Filipino Culture and Christian Liturgy' *Concilium* 102 (1977), pp. 62-71: 'Liturgical Feasts and the Seasons of the Year' *Concilium* 142 (1982), pp. 31-36.

14. See particularly the volumes on *The Use of Hindu, Buddhist and Muslim Scriptures in the Liturgy* (never printed in English, n. 132 in other language editions), *Liturgy and Cultural Religious Traditions* (n. 102) (1977), *The Times of Celebration* (n. 142/162) (1981) and *Liturgy: A Creative Tradition* (n. 162/182) (1983).

Edward Schillebeeckx

You Cannot Arbitrarily Make Something of the Gospel!

THE VERY first issue of *Concilium* devoted to dogmatic theology was basically a consideration of the theological themes contained in the Second Vatican Council's Dogmatic Constitution, *Lumen Gentium*, on the Church. It also contained an explicit statement about the direction that would be followed in those dogmatic issues. That was to be a reflection, in the light of the problems presented by contemporary man's experience of his own existence, about the reality of God who had, in revealing himself in Jesus Christ, at the same time revealed man to himself.

This in fact happened in the first nineteen dogmatic issues. The reality of God was discussed in two issues: the 'personally divine' aspect of God and the 'impersonally divine' aspect (1977, 3) and *God as Father* (1981, 3). God's self-revelation was discussed on several occasions (1967, 1; 1970, 1; 1978, 1). This self-revelation as having been definitively accomplished in Jesus Christ as the absolute and redemptive nearness of God was considered at least once (1966, 1). That absolute nearness of God in the man Jesus was also particularly stressed at a time when men were longing for liberation (1974, 3) and there is now a strong reaction against an a-political and even anti-political Christology. This tendency is reflected in the theme of Jesus as the Son of God (1982, 3).

Other aspects of this question that have been considered are: man's being revealed to himself by God's revelation of himself (1983, 3), human salvation as mediated by the world (1965, 1) and by the Church's sacraments (1968, 1), eschatological salvation (1969, 1; 1979, 3) and all these questions seen as reconciliation (1971, 1) of man who is failing and sometimes impotent (1976, 3) in a world containing demonic elements (1975, 3).

The contemporary Church has also frequently been considered in the dogmatic issues of *Concilium*: as a sign of salvation for the world (1965, 1), as struggling with internal tensions in the process of evolving new ways of thinking and acting (1970, 1), in dealing with new experiences (1978, 3; 1967, 1), in its own official structures (1972, 3; 1973, 1) and in connection with papal infallibility and with the priestly office and pastoral workers (1980, 3).

It should be clear, then, from this brief survey that the plan outlined in the first dogmatic issue of *Concilium* has to a very great extent been carried out in the nineteen issues.[1] Between 1965 and 1973, the classical sections or separate theological disciplines were for the most part preserved and those writing for the dogmatic issues tended to choose themes to do with the Church and to write 'academic' theology. *Concilium* was given a new face in 1973, although, because of the timing of the journal, this was not seen until 1974, when readers became aware of a distinct change. Although the different sections, such as Dogma, Moral Theology and Liturgy, continued as a substructure, they receded into the background and each issue was concentrated on one theme, each theme being dealt with in an inter-disciplinary manner.

From 1974 onwards, then, the dogmatic issues became much more closely related to man's problems 'in the world'. The point of reference was no longer the Second Vatican Council, which gave the journal its name of *Concilium*, but the situation in the world and the Church since the Council. It is in fact only since the Council that the official structures in the world have become so radically democratised. There have also been many student riots since that time. We have become aware of the poverty and hunger of two-thirds of the world's population. We are increasingly concerned about the way in which our natural resources are being used up. The oil crisis occurred after the Council and we are troubled about increasing unemployment in the West, yet unrestricted economic expansion seems to have only evil consequences. The East-West conflict is often overshadowed by the contrast between North and South. The central European churches are in a much weaker position. During the 1970s, we in the West became very alarmed about our own prosperity and as a result politically apathetic and despairing. Periods of crisis almost always produce radical movements and counter-movements. Some people seek refuge in the inner life and become a-political. Others find salvation in action and often resort to demonstrations and even violence. In extreme cases, this may lead to a complete loss of the inner life and of all desire to preserve one's own and other people's humanity.

There is, in other words, an enormous contrast between the times in which we are now living and 1962-65, the years when the Second Vatican Council took place. Then we were living in a world which had just surmounted the chaos of the Second World War and had been made very confident by increasing economic prosperity. Reading the Council's Pastoral Constitution, *Gaudium et Spes*, on the Church in the Modern World now, almost twenty years after its publication, we are struck by its almost naïve optimism. The Roman Catholic Church defined the part that it could play and the contribution that it could make in the world's great movement towards prosperity and welfare in that classical document. Since the 1970s, however, we have passed through and are still in the throes of a severe economic crisis and the cry of 'surrender' is heard everywhere. Bad though it may be in the West, the Third World is even more seriously affected by this crisis.

Vatican II was, of course, also a council of protest and dissension. It expressed the reaction on the part of the liberal Church against the remnants of a feudal and monarchistic structure in the Church. One of the most important results of this was the emphasis on collegiality in the government of the Church. It was in fact only through the Council that the great achievements of the French Revolution and civil liberty were accepted officially by the Church. By an irony of history, it was just when the Church accepted tolerance, religious freedom, ecumenical openness and freedom of conscience that society began to criticise the new forms of slavery created by the liberal bourgeoisie.

It is interesting to note that Bishop Wojtyła's point of view, to judge from his interventions during the Second Vatican Council, was different in almost every case not only from that of the majority of the bishops, but also from that of the small minority. There was a period of euphoria that was almost triumphalistic for a few years after the Council, but that has now almost completely vanished. On the one hand, there has not been enough time for the Council to bear ripe fruit. On the other hand, approximately half of the world's bishops, namely those who did not personally take part in the Council, regard Vatican II as a set of historical documents, like those of Nicaea or Trent, that have to be studied. They have not experienced the Council itself or the inspiration of participating in it.

Because of this, Vatican II has not been the point of reference for *Concilium* generally and for its dogmatic issues in particular since 1974. We have in fact taken the present-day, post-conciliar situation in the Church and the world as our starting-point and that is, of course, quite different from the situation during the Council. The issues devoted to dogmatic theology have become quite noticeably more related to the contemporary reality. This does not mean that they deal with ephemeral matters or fleeting fashions. They are rather concerned with the essential problems of humanity in the world of today. This was strikingly reflected in the dogmatic issue that appeared in 1983. The theme then was 'political holiness and martyrdom' in the 1980s. In the issue devoted to failing man (1976, 3), an attempt was made to analyse and to reflect theologically about the spirit of resignation and even defeatism in the 1970s, after the student revolts and a widespread acceptance of the fact that the structures were much more tenacious than had been thought.

Is it possible to distinguish any clear orientations for the future in the nineteen dogmatic issues published so far? One very obvious fact is that 'dogmatic theology'—which is, incidentally, not to be found exclusively in the dogmatic numbers—is in a state of movement. It is becoming increasingly clear that many 'dogmatic' problems cannot be solved in an abstract and purely 'dogmatic' way. There is also the urgent question as to how a community that believes in God's salvation in Jesus Christ can make sure that that confession of faith has an influence on society. It seems preferable not to regard God as true rather than to believe in a God who is inhuman or who enslaves man. We shall get no further if we make such abstract pronouncements as 'Jesus is the Son of God' or 'salvation can only be found in the name of Jesus', above all if we do this while at the same time failing to show how that Christian confession of faith functions socially and politically.

Since 1969, following the great movements of contestation, a clearer insight into the implications of this has emerged from the issues devoted to dogmatic theology. Broadly speaking, it is possible to say that existentialism and phenomenology were reflected in the earlier dogmatic theology of *Concilium*, while the later articles, to some extent since 1968 and quite markedly since 1974, were critical of society. This tendency towards the criticism of society emerges quite clearly from a comparison between the issues devoted to Jesus. One early issue (1966, 1) is quite noticeably existentialist, a second (1974, 3) deals with the theme of Jesus and human freedom and a third (1982, 3), to which can be added a fourth on the theme of following Jesus to death (1983, 3), considers the oppressive and repressive structures of our society. What is particularly interesting in this context, however, is that the two directors had to admit in their editorial in that very early issue (1966, 1) with its strongly existentialist orientation that the real problems that had arisen 'in recent years' has not been sufficiently taken into account. The change in emphasis in Christology was at that time confined to the problems raised by Bultmann's existential interpretation of the Bible and the arguments for and against it.

FUTURE PERSPECTIVES

From 1984 onwards, *Concilium* will cease to appear ten times each year. The reason for producing only six issues in future is to explore one theme more deeply each time. We hope to concentrate on such questions as: With whom and for who are we doing theology? Who is the real subject of our theologising? Is *Concilium* simply a mouthpiece for academic, professional theologians? Theology is becoming increasingly involved in the tension between the world universalism of the kingdom of God and a concentration on Christology. A recurrent theme in recent issues of *Concilium* has been universality and particularity (cultural regionality). But in this respect, we are still only at the beginning. It is even possible to detect signs that the 'Third World' and the 'Western' theologies are not really attuned to each other, in other words, that there is no intercommunication between them. Every branch of theology has its own context and we have to remain conscious of that by maintaining dialogue and remaining open to true universality. The latter must never be allowed to become abstract, even if that is enlightened. True universality is always mediated by particularity. If *Concilium* avoided critical confrontation and discouraged mutual listening it would become no more than a theological supermarket in which different religious views were offered like goods imported from various countries. It would be, in other words, a meaningless platform without any specific tendency. This may sometimes have happened, but it is certainly something that we want to avoid in the future, since pluralism, presented in this way, is not a blessing, but simply an expression of a liberal free market, an uncommitted and unproductive event. We have passed through the euphoria of the 'slogan of pluralism' and now we have, without declining into a new form of dogmatism, to study the limits of Christian pluralism. You cannot arbitrarily make something of the Gospel, even in the political sense! The Gospel is radical. It is true that the radical nature of the Gospel has to be expressed in a contemporary way in new, contemporary situations that are often more complex and ambivalent than in the past, but it is something that Christians cannot avoid.

It should be possible to present the Christological concept of the one God of all peoples and cultures in a clearer and more meaningful way if we remember that what God wants above all is to save mankind and human history and, within that framework, the individual as well. This means that any form of privatisation and cultural monocentrism must be seriously criticised. However much it tries to escape from European and North American monocentrism, *Concilium* is still exposed to the danger of its specific strength, that of being an international journal, becoming its main weakness.

One important fact is that most of the authors writing for *Concilium* have so far been more than fifty years old and many of them are more than sixty. Only a small minority were born after the Second World War. This is a situation that has to be remedied.

Concilium also has the task of stressing in the future even more than it has done in the past the fact that Jesus of Nazareth, who is the same as the 'Christ of faith', confronts us at the deepest level with the question of God. It has therefore to emphasise that we are confronted with a God who is concerned with man and who also wants us to be concerned with mankind. The emphasis, in other words, has to be on the biblical vision of the kingdom of God.

This points at one and the same time to both the mystical and the political implication of following Jesus. My co-director of the dogmatic section of *Concilium* (or the section concerned with the 'teaching of faith'), J.-B. Metz, would join me in saying that the period of self-legitimation of Christianity is past and that we are now enteing the period of liberation. The messianic praxis of 'following Jesus' (not the *imitatio*, but the *sequela Jesu*) is at the same time a liberation from destructive poverty and inhuman oppression and repression. At the same time, however, it is in opposing evil and innocent suffering that the source of all liberation can be experienced and that source is the God of liberation, the promoter of everything that is good and the opposer of everything that is evil and therefore also the source of all prayer and mysticism.

Translated by David Smith

Note

1. The directors of the dogmatic issues have been (1) from 1965 to 1971, E. Schillebeeckx and A. B. Willems, two dogmatic theologians; (2) from 1973 to 1979, B. van Iersel and E. Schillebeeckx, an exegete and a dogmatic theologian; (3) from 1980 onwards, J.-B. Metz and E. Schillebeeckx, a fundamental theologian and a dogmatic theologian. This is clear enough evidence that, since 1973, preference has been given in the dogmatic section to a concentrated theologically interdisciplinary approach.

Virgil Elizondo and Norbert Greinacher

Stages of Practical Theology

PRE-VATICAN II

EVEN THOUGH there were some *avant-garde* movements, for most of the Church
'pastoral theology' was the ordinary knowledge of the ordinary parish priest—how to
enter baptisms into the records, how to calculate mass stipends, regulations concerning
the sacraments and Christian burial . . . etc.

Although great breakthroughs were being made by men like Jungmann in Austria,
Hoffinger in Manila, Nebreda in Japan, and several others, for most of the Church and
of theologians, pastoral theology had to do with the simple running of the parish—it was
clerical and mechanical. The subsequent development of *Concilium* reflects the
evolution of Church practice from Vatican Council II to the present irruption of the
Third World.

1. VATICAN II

The great evolution of pastoral theology is best exemplified by the first editorial of
the 1965 issue of Pastoral Theology written by K. Rahner:

> Since the function of theology in the Church is to lay down the basis of the
> Church's self-awareness in a scientific manner, it cannot limit itself to the unfolding
> of the permanent factors in the history of the Church. The present and the future of
> the Church, too, fall necessarily within the scope of theological thought. Only
> *pastoral* theology can undertake this task. But it can only do so if we no longer leave
> it to collect and transmit norms, regulations and pastoral experiences for use by the
> clergy. The life of the Church is not confined to clerical contributions but all
> members of the Church are involved in this. Pastoral theology, therefore, can no
> longer be limited to the pastoral functions of the clergy. It must become 'practical
> theology' in the true sense of the word (Vol. 3, p. 1).

He goes on to state that practical theology involves all the members of the Church in
the self-realisation of the Church in the world. Because of constantly changing
contemporary situations, critical sociological and scientific analysis will be demanded.
'This is vital because the contemporary situation is precisely that moment of salvation
history in which God makes us here and now responsible for the realisation of the
Church' (*ibid.*, p. 1).

Rahner's contribution was certainly radical and far reaching. It brought out the responsibility of all Christians in the task of the Church. It was not just up to clerics and religious but for all the baptised to bring about the realisation of the Church. Furthermore, he brought out the need to read the signs of the times in a critical way. It was precisely in the here and now that God was bringing about salvation. There are no absolutes or eternal answers to the new situations which arise in the world.

It is in this spirit that the first volumes of Practical Theology of *Concilium* have been produced. They dealt with exclusively intra-ecclesial questions in the context of the contemporary world. But they did not go beyond the intra-ecclesial questions to the questions of the Church and the world or even beyond that to the Church in the world. Hence it is not surprising to see the first issues dealing with a study of practical theology itself and the role of sociology, the mission, pastoral analysis of the situation created by modern atheism, preaching, ministry and life of the priest today, catechesis, democratisation in the Church and reform of the Church. These issues dealt with many pressing and contemporary questions and challenges facing the post-Vatican II Church.

In 1966, I was named Archdiocesan Director of Religious Education. It was the period immediately after the Council and during the beginnings of *Concilium*. I must confess that although I was very aware of the literature of pastoral renewal that was coming out of Manila, Paris, Ottawa, Mexico City and Madrid, I was not aware of *Concilium* at that time. I make this personal observation for two reasons: Upon examining those back issues in preparation for this issue, I certainly wish I had been aware of them. They would have been of very great assistance in my assignment to bring about the renewal of the religious education programme and of seminary education so as to bring it in line with the teaching of Vatican II.

The second reason is that looking back upon those exciting and euphoric days of the beginning of the renewal it is incredible how *Concilium* caught the core issues that were facing the Church of the 1960s and early 1970s. Many of the articles which appeared then continue to be most relevant in the life of the Church today. The articles were exploratory, creative and provocative. In fact, considering the Vatican I mentality which had become like second nature to the Church, they were revolutionary breakthroughs. They opened the doors and paved the way for the concrete implementation of Vatican II Church life.

Subjects such as catechetics and preaching which had always been delegated a very subordinate role in the seminary curriculum or in the preparation of religious men and women preparing for the teaching of theological and secular sciences now started to take a first place in the list of priorities. D. Grasso's book on the theology of preaching became an immediate classic within Catholic circles. We had the sacraments while the Protestants had the preaching. Preaching sounded so Protestant, yet it started to emerge as the very heart of priestly ministry. A Copernican revolution within the sacramental life of the Church was rapidly taking place.

Catechetics could no longer be left for those who had nothing else to do. It appeared as the very essence of the life of the Church. The Institut Catholique de Paris trained many of the teams who brought about a complete renewal of grass-roots catechetics throughout Latin America, India and Asia. Institutes such as Lumen Vitae in Brussels, East Asian Pastoral Institute in Manila, Sedes Sapientiae in Mexico City, Institute Catequistico Latino Americano in Manizales (Colombia), started to flourish and to give a very serious and creative approach to catechesis.

But as we returned to the sources of Christianity and became aware that the pastoral mission of the Church was for all baptised Christians and not just for clerics or religious, the whole question of the democratisation of the Church arose. Collegiality was not limited to the bishops but extended to all levels of Church life. This was easy to say theologically but it brought serious structural questions to the Church. These were treated in 1971 and in 1972. These issues are still being struggled with today and will continue to challenge the structural life of the Church as it seeks to reform itself continually in the light of its foundational sources. In fact the 1971 issues on *Democratisation of the Church* and the 1972 issue on the *Reform of the Church* continue to be prophetic in a Church which for centuries has understood its foundational structure through the monarchical culture of the middle ages. Will today's Church be able to reconvert to its own earliest tradition? These are probably even more live issues today than they were ten years ago.

2. POST-VATICAN II DEVELOPMENTS

In 1973, *Concilium* decided to embark on a 'new face'. It seems that the influence of *Pacem in Terris* of John XXIII, *Populorum Progressio* of Paul VI, the Conclusions of the Latin American Bishops' Conference of Medellín of 1968, and the Bishops Synod on Justice in 1971 all helped to give the issue of practical theology of *Concilium* not only a new face but a more far-reaching orientation. From being concerned with intra-ecclesial questions, it nows passes on to deal with questions of the relationship of the Church to the world. The Church could not avoid questions of the relationship of the Church to the world. The Church could not stand idle or on the sidelines of the pressing questions of the world. What were Christians to do when faced with hunger, disease, poverty and exploitation? Is the work of Christians simply almsgiving, or does it demand a critical and active involvement in the transformation of the market-place?

There seems to be a growing consensus of the need of Christians to be involved politically, or even the conscious non-involvement will serve as a neutrality of the status quo. The question is rather a pragmatic one: In what way are we to be involved as Christians? It is here that N. Greinacher's understanding of practical theology begins to make a significant contribution to the overall direction of *Concilium*. The first issue of 1973 on the political commitment of the Christian community is a concrete working out of his theory of the bipolar tension between theory and practice. In the opening editorial on determining the role of Christians in political actions he states:

> But the inductive method alone is not enough. In deciding the question of political involvement in relation to the Christian community it is absolutely vital to analyse the situation and function of the community within the society as a whole. This provides us with important criteria that will affect the attitude of the community. But over and above this and precisely in the process of deciding upon these issues the community has to reflect about its origins in Jesus and upon its own understanding of itself as a Christian community. In this respect different communities and different theologians come up with different answers. . . . But in other respects it will not be possible to answer the problem of the Christian community's political involvement purely deductively. Instead, a solution will above all have to be sought on the basis of actual experience within the actual situation (1973, p. 9).

Practical theology is not just to explain or legitimise the actual practice of the Church but it must reflect critically on the actual practice of the Church in the light of socio-historical conditions of the time and of the reality of Jesus. The ongoing question for practical theology is: How is the Church helping to bring about liberation of the human person? Hence, practical theology will not only explore the life and practice of the Church, but it will equally offer a questioning critique for the on-going evolution and purification of the Church.

Beginning this new face of *Concilium* I really do not understand why the editors immediately treated the experience and rituals of death. Maybe it was symbolic to begin with the end of life—death—and then work towards movements for life. However, the issue on death was quite interesting in the series of the new face.

The 1975 issue dealing with *Basic Christian Communities* might well be called a frontier issue on several counts. It deals with the growing phenomenon of basic Christian communities. I say that this is a frontier issue because it makes several breakthroughs in contemporary pastoral theology. First of all, the basic Christian communities are much more concerned with Christian living than with Christian dogmas. Their concern is with personalising the Gospel, making an existential response to the demands of the Gospel in these particular social circumstances, and working for the transformation of the environment.

They are frontier because they mark the end of a clerically centred pastoral ministry and the beginning of one that is centred on the ministry of the baptised Christians. The basic Christian communities are not generally anticlerical or antihierarchical, but they do transcend the divisions (distinctions) of clergy-laity—they are neither anticlerical nor clergy dependent. If the clergy is around, they are welcomed, if they are not around, they are not missed.

This type of Christian community raises profound theological questions in relation to the official ministers of the Church, in particular with the officially commissioned ministers of the Eucharist and of reconciliation. Whereas the present-day basic Christian communities are not trying to play priest, the very nature of their faith celebrations raises the question of their relationship to the official liturgies of the Church. The Latin American Bishops' Conference meeting in Puebla in 1979 would later on wrestle with the question of the faith celebrations of the basic faith community but it will not solve the question—it remains an open question.

They are frontier because they are emerging not out of ecclesial legislation from the top but from the response of the people to the invitation of the Word of God. They are one of the breakthroughs of the Spirit in the present age. As the editorial of *Concilium* points out, they are giving a new face to the Church and allowing the people to come forth with new aspects of Church which the clergy would not be capable of bringing about because of their interiorised clerical culture of the past generations.

In 1977, *Concilium* directed its Church-World dialogue to the ever-present yet ever-evasive question of poverty. 'No effective action will be taken against hunger as long as there is no general acceptance of its scandal' (F. Bastos de Avila, p. 1). Pastoral ministry cannot just give alms or take care of the destitute. As part of its prophetic mission it must denounce 'the iniquity of concentration of goods in the hands of the few, the injustices in unequal distribution of resources which the humblest have helped with their sweat and their blood to create' (*ibid.*, p. 6).

Yet the Church must go further than just ministering to the poor or even raising its prophetic voice to denounce injustice. As Gustavo Gutiérrez points out in his issue: 'Perhaps we should go further and say that the preaching of the Gospel will be truly liberating when the poor themselves are the preachers' (p. 15). This is a radical inversion for the Church, its missionary-pastoral activity and for *Concilium*. The Church-World dialogue has usually been carried out among the élite of society—especially the élites of Europe. Gutiérrez brings out that the world's poor—the silent and absent ones of history and society—are to be the main interlocutors and preachers of the Word. This view is not just an invention of Gutiérrez. It is a rediscovery of the very originality of the Basileia of the New Testament (Bockmann, p. 36). The ecclesial implications of this turning of things inside out are quite vast. It is a complete displacement of the privileged place of theology and of the very agents of the theologising process. As Muñoz brings out, there are two models of Church functioning side by side. 'On the one hand, there is

C

the model of the great institutional Church, with its sociological and cultural centre outside the world of the poor, in the rich sectors of the country and the rich nations of the world; a Church that values discipline more and seeks greater functional cohesion; that practices organised aid to the poor; a Church with the power to negotiate the political and military authorities and exercise some pressure on them in order to obtain a amelioration of the social conditions brought about by the regime; a Church that teaches doctrine with authority and can make itself heard through the mass media of communication.

'The other model is that of the communications-network Church, with its sociological and cultural centre in the world of the poor, among the poor who make up the bulk of the population of this country [Chile] and of the poor countries of the world; a Church that values fraternity more and looks for a greater sharing of responsibility; that lives and preaches solidarity in the midst of the people, filling its role of prophetic denunciation of injustice, discreetly maybe, but still accepting the concomitant risks, so as to awaken a consciousness of their dignity in the poor together with hope for a better world; a Church that, in and from the world of the poor, seeks to bear witness to the Gospel, generally without disposing of any means of communication beyond person to person contact' (Muñoz, p. 82).

This pivotal volume on poverty prepares the way for the 1978 issue on *Evangelisation in the World Today* which dared to pose and explore the all-important question: Are Western missioners, by the very fact of being of the colonial and dominant West, capable of announcing the liberating Good News to the non-Western peoples who are, generally speaking, the poor of the world: 'Is it [evangelisation] perhaps so laden with the guilt of centuries that it has lost its credibility?' (p. vii). As with the previous issue on poverty, this issue's great contribution is that it begins to repose the most fundamental question of the pastoral ministry of the Church. It poses it from the perspective of God's chosen ones: the poor and the marginated of the world.

As Gutiérrez brought out the theological role of the poor in the preaching of the Word, in 1978 Father Amalorpavadaas of India brings out the need for the Gospel to be transmitted by way of inculturation. For many of the Third World countries, this is the core ecclesial question. How to be Christian without being Western or without being considered by the rest of the Church to be inferior and uneducated because they were not Western? Is there any way out of the Western tutelage of the Universal Church? Will the dominant Church of the West ever allow such a displacement of theology and ministry?

1979 and 1980 formed an interesting evolution in the thinking and concerns of *Concilium*: From *The Church and the Rights of* Man (emphasis my own) to *Women in a Men's Church?* they were both burning pastoral issues. The evolution even from men, wishing to include women, to an issue devoted to the question of women is quite an evolution in itself. In a time when men and women were disappearing left and right in Catholic countries, when they were being arrested, tortured and mutilated, the Church cannot remain silent and passive. And beyond that, what are we to do about 50 per cent of the Church's membership who are excluded from full participation in the sacrament of life and ministry of the Church simply because they are women? They were touchy subjects but in honesty to the Word of God they had to be treated by a Church that confesses to be the carrier of the very word which brings liberation to all.

3. AN ECCLESIAL INVERSION

The theological shift of doing theology from the recognised centres of authority and learning, to doing theology from the margins of civilisation which was already

67987

mentioned in some of the articles of earlier issues, emerges in a strong and explicit way in the issue on 'Women' and especially in a 1981 issue on *Tensions Between the Churches of the First World and the Third World*.

We might well see in these two issues the beginning of the third era of the Practical Theology issue of *Concilium*. It evolves from the strong emphasis on intra-ecclesia issues to the question of the relationship between the Church (universal) and the problems of the world, to the relationship between the church (local) within its own cultural region and the demands of the Gospel in the world community. In this third era, the voices of the poor and the marginated speak for themselves. The local churches of the margins of the old Christian world now begin to speak in a universal language. They speak from the depths of their pains and struggles but their message certainly has a universal implication for all. A new view of Catholicity begins to emerge, that is the universality that emerges out of the particular and well-defined situation of poverty, exploitation and margination.

There is no one universal Christian culture and the universal Church exists only in the mystery of the particular. Only in the dialogue of the fellowship of local churches can each local church, including the Church of Rome, be liberated from its own cultural idols and blind spots. In this new awareness of the tension between the local and the universal Church, Rome continues to be the centre of Christian unity but it should no longer be the totalitarian and domineering centre which imposes uniformity upon others. The very teaching of *Christus Dominus* and *Lumen Gentium* leads us to a new understanding of the mystery of the local-universal Church. Furthermore, the traditionally marginated and silent churches of the so-called Third World begin to speak not only with an astounding vigour but equally from a newly experienced position of equality. European theologians are no longer regarded as the universal masters but as the limited and conditioned Christian thinkers of the West. They have much to say but they equally have much to learn from the other thinkers of the world.

This trend to provide a forum for the fellowship of churches continues in the 1982 issue *Religion and Churches in Eastern Europe*. It was a brief look and the editors more than anyone else realised that it was serious but that it fell short of being adequate. There is so much more going on in Eastern Europe than we in the West have ever suspected. Yet it was important to hear the voices of the churches of Eastern Europe.

In the final issue leading to this anniversary issue, we tackled the contemporary question of the *Church and Peace*. An attempt was made not just to quickly join the Western world's bandwagon, but to give a voice for people with more violent and pressing present-day threats to life than the nuclear bomb. The West is worried and concerned because its own life is being threatened but it still remains blissfully ignorant and unconcerned as the West continues to kill in the Third World through the weapons of dangerous and lethal fertilisers and baby formulas, dumping of radioactive wastes in the rivers of the Third World, withholding grain and food to maintain economic stability while 40,000 babies die per day because of malnutrition; using dangerous and untested birth control methods with people of the Third World without them knowing about it or giving their consent; sending more and more military aid to Guatemala, Argentina and Chile, El Salvador and other militaries of the world and thus continuing to kill the poor and the suffering who are simply struggling for a more human existence. We do not send them agricultural aid to grow their products but only military aid to kill those who are struggling to grow their products and initiate something new. In many ways, the West kills thousands per day and no one seems to be too concerned. But the nuclear threat awakened in us an immediate concern—our own life was now being threatened. This made all the difference in the world. The issue on *Peace* attempted to address the complexity of the issues of peacemaking. For authentic peace is not just the absence of war but the initiation of a new world order of true justice and harmony. Christians are not so much called to oppose the war as they are called upon to be actively engaged in the total work of peacemaking.

As I have gone through the past issues of *Concilium*, I was delighted to see the evolution. All three moments continue to be important since the Church could not serve or confront the world if it did not develop its own inner life and ministry. We must continue to be concerned about the life of faith if the faithful are to be the leaven in the world. Hence, intra-ecclesial questions continue to be timely and important. Yet, without a serious opening to the world, ecclesial questions can be reduced to navel gazing—as they often are. Church must always be reminded that it is called into existence in order to be of service to the world. But even as we look at the socio-political-economic questions of the world, in a rapidly shrinking world we must always be aware of the viewpoint of others—especially the marginated and the powerless of the world. By the very nature of its originality, the Church must take a lead in providing a podium for the powerless and voiceless of the world. For not only must they be heard, but theologically speaking it is from among their ranks that the Gospel must be preached to all the world. They, the nothing of the world, are to be the new teachers of the new creation.

Finally, in the new issue that is being prepared, Practical Theology completes its circle and returns to the intra-ecclesial question of the transmission of faith to the next generation. This is certainly not a going back but a complete and integral concern for the total life and practice of the Church. The Church must serve its own people in that which is unique to it, the proclamation of the Gospel. But as a Christian community we must be concerned with the suffering and the needs of the world. And as a world community we must go from the dichotomy of dominant and dominated to the fellowship of being real partners with all nations and all churches in the common enterprise of creating a new world. This threefold task of the Church has been well addressed by *Concilium* it is our hope that we will continue to do so.

Johann-Baptist Metz

Facing a Torn World

I

UNLIKE THE other sections of this journal, 'Fundamental Theology' did not appear from the beginning under its own subject heading. Until the end of 1972 it was described either by the not unambiguous label 'Borderline questions' or by the programmatic title 'Church and world'. Since 1973, and now under the editorship of J.-P. Jossua and myself, it has appeared exclusively under the title 'Fundamental Theology'.[1]

1. Justice should first be done to the programmatic significance of the title 'Church and world', which encapsulated the philosophy of the section from the beginning. The first volume (1965) appealed explicitly to the new understanding of the world and the new relationship between Church and world which emerged in the Vatican II Pastoral Constitution *Gaudium et Spes*. This, it seems to me, is the impulse which this section above all sought to pick up from the still recent council, to protect and to give further theological development. Finally, what emerged particularly in this Constitution— though naturally in other of the council's constitutions as well, such as the Constitution on the Church, *Lumen Gentium*—was an understanding of the world, and specifically of the world-wide Church, which can be legitimately be described as 'new' and which in many of its impulses was in advance of the understanding of the world and the Church implicit in the generality of theological writing. I am thinking here above all of that view of the Church which for the first time revealed the world with its social divisions and cultural polycentrism as internal to the one Church.

It is therefore no accident that our section in particular firstly treated the social and political issues of our modern world as fundamental issues of theology (as early as 1968) and ecclesiology (see 1971). Secondly, the lines of inquiry which met around the programmatic title 'Church and world' made a first attempt to breach the traditional Eurocentrism of our theological and ecclesiological awareness. The volumes of the 1970s were filled increasingly by articles, situational analyses and questioning from the churches of what is called the Third World. This development was encouraged in the realisation that from now on the Catholic Church no longer simply maintained dependencies in the lands beyond Europe and North America, in other words that it no longer simply 'had' a Third World Church, but 'was'—in terms of empirical ecclesiology—a Third World Church with a historical origin in Western Europe. Even when this was discussed under headings such as *Christianity and Socialism* (1977) and *Christianity and the Bourgeoisie* (1979), implicit in these and other issues of the section was an awareness of a new relationship between Church and world and a new phase of the 'world Church'. The 1980 issue on the universality of Christianity also documented an awareness of this situation and the new problems it created for the universal message of Christianity.

2. Of course we tried from the beginning not to treat even the so-called 'borderline questions' as marginal to theology, but to approach them by means of a productive interdisciplinary confrontation with scientific and ideological positions in today's world, marked as it is by so-called Western rationality. It was fully in accord with this principle that I should have shared responsibility for this section until 1972 with the natural scientist W. Bröker and the philosopher W. Oelmüller. The subjects dealt with in this period invariably touched on questions connected with the fundamentals of the Christian faith and in this sense fell within the domain of fundamental theology. In these issues theology sought to come to terms critically and productively with typical and influential forms of contemporary atheism (1966), with questions formulated in predominantly scientific terms in the treatment of the topic of 'Evolution' (1967), with positions taken in the human sciences in relation to the question of the existence and interpretation of evil in the world (1970), but above all with sociological and political issues in the attempt to define the role of the Church and theology in a changed socio-political environment (1968).

These attempts to come to terms with other disciplines also brought to light what might be called—though with great caution—the permanent 'apologetic' character of theology. 'Apologetic' here is naturally not to be understood in the sense of those defensive ideologies which use logical short-cuts and minor dishonesties; it does not mean the insistence on being right which has perhaps often dominated apologetics as a defensive branch of theology. No, what I mean is the 'apologetic' character of fundamental theology which makes it want to reveal the inherent power of the faith to give practical answers. Theology is faced with a particular challenge from modern cognitive systems. It knows that many of these systems are cognitively far from neutral towards religion and theology. Many of them see themselves, though with varying degrees of explicitness, as so-called meta-theories of religion and theology. For them theology can be completely analysed and subsumed within a more general theoretical system. Theology's response to such theories cannot be to seek a foundation and justification in a further attempt to produce a more general 'pure theory' from its own resources. In order to avoid the risk of a speculative infinite regression, which would inevitably have to be broken off arbitrarily at some point, it must look for its basis in terms of *a return to the subjects of faith and their practice*. In other words, it must regard itself in a very precise sense as a practical explanatory discipline. The so-called relationship of theory and practice, which seeks to uncover the practical and subjective foundation of all theological wisdom, is inherent in this sort of theology. This was brought out with ever greater clarity in the issues devoted more explicitly to the situation and tasks of fundamental theology, from about 1968 on.

3. Over the twenty years during which it has appeared it has been a constant aim of this section to deal explicitly with issues related to the character of our discipline, fundamental theology, and with the changing understanding of what fundamental theology might be. The 1969 volume attempted to draw a balance of the situation of contemporary fundamental theology, following a discussion of the discipline in 1968 as a political-practical hermeneutic of the Gospel—under the newly current title 'Political Theology'. In 1978 we discussed where (and by whom) theology was now beginning to be done, an investigation confronting fundamental theology not least as a result of exchanges with the attempts to develop a theology of liberation in the Third World, particularly in Latin America. In the issues for 1977 (*Christianity and Socialism*) and 1979 (*Christianity and the Bourgeoisie*) the significance of the issues of the subject and of practice for fundamental theology were discussed in real historical and social contexts.

Individual issues from this period, dealing with 'classical' questions in fundamental theology, developed the interests mentioned here with varying degrees of intensity: the issue on the Church (1971), the treatment of the theme of 'Changes in the Debate about God' (1972), and the question of immortality in the face of our modern, so-called secularised, world's myths of finitude (1975).

The issues for 1974 (The Recovery of Sensuality) and those for 1973 and 1976 (The Crisis of Religious Language, Theology and Literature), finally, are related to another fundamental issue in contemporary theology, the theory of culture and society. This is the question of the relationship between myth and rationality in a world shaped by the processes of the Enlightenment and of secularisation. The articles in these issues show a particular sensitivity to the inner dialectic of these processes, to the theological and cultural dangers of a radical theoretical rejection of myth (such as that attempted by the demythologisation school), and to the dangers of a rationalistic reduction of the rationality of theology and an associated depreciation of the cognitive inputs of memories and symbols. Examples from this area include the discussion on 'narrative theology' in the 1973 issue and the issue devoted to Nietzsche (1980), which, significantly, attracted attention outside professional philosophical circles.

II

Some readers may have the feeling that in all this we have stuck our fingers into too many pies. Some theologians, who regard the familiar subdivisions of theology as untouchable, will regret the intrusion of fundamental theology into other disciplines and may feel that this has not infrequently been paid for in semantic confusion. Nevertheless the situation of a theology which today regards itself as fundamental theology is complex in a particular way. I have already referred to its 'practical' character. There is also a further factor. The cognitive obviousness of theology was dealt a severe blow by the processes by which the modern era developed, notably the critique of its foundations in historicism and in the most varied forms of bourgeois and Marxist critique of religion. Questions of historical dependence and social interests are no longer outside systematic theology. Nor can they be pushed to the fringes of theology by any apologetic sleight of hand. They concern the central process of theology! A fundamental theology in our time must take account of this, and this is what we have sought to do over these years—of course only sporadically and by no means always adequately.

The issues of these last twenty years, then, may be seen as evidence that theology is making its contribution to that apologia of hope which is part of our Christian life. This task was performed in an awareness of the world of social conflicts which has become the Church's primary environment, and in an awareness of the new relationship between Church and world which may perhaps be described as the transition from a Church consisting of Europe and North America with a single cultural centre to a culturally polycentric world Church. Our journal above all should increasingly be a forum and a school for Christian practice and doing theology in this new situation.

Translated by Francis McDonagh

Note

1. For the year 1979-80 I transferred to the Dogmatics section and Claude Geffré took my place.

David Tracy

'Project X': Retrospect and Prospect

1. RETROSPECTIVE: DISCERNING THE SIGNS OF THE TIMES

SINCE 1973 with the beginning of the 'new face' of *Concilium*, readers of this journal witnessed the emergence of a new category: Project 'X'. For ten years now, the tenth issue of *Concilium* has addressed a set of questions that do not fit easily into any of the other more familiar classifications of theology. The fact that a particular question does not 'fit' within our usual categories nor within more usual modes of inquiry does not mean that this question is not a major one demanding theological response. Indeed, in one sense, Project 'X' has seen its principal task to be the need to try to discern the signs of the times—to discern those issues, questions, movements, and demands which suggest why theology cannot in our time be 'business as usual'. The concerns and often the content of some issues of Project 'X' (see, especially, the 1974 issue entitled *The Mystical and Political Dimension of Christian Faith*) have had great impact in the ensuing years on all theology. For the centrality of the mystico-political dimension of *all* Christian faith and *all* Christian theology has now come to be widely admitted by most forms of theology—whether they name themselves 'liberation' or 'political' theologies or not.

An issue like that 1974 issue functioned exactly as the editorial board hoped Project 'X' could function: to articulate, to render explicit, a major set of concerns which should influence all theology and all Christian faith. Other single issues of Project 'X'—like the 1973 issue on the crisis of humanism and the 1980 issue on the import of recent debates across the disciplines on the meaning of the central category 'religion' for Christian theology itself—have also served to highlight central questions for any theology which need to be addressed if theology is to fulfil its difficult task of discerning the signs of our demanding times.

Alongside those central questions which cut across all the theological disciplines (the mystico-political dimension of all Christian faith, the crisis of humanism, the debate on the meaning of religion), Project 'X' has also attempted to discern those signs by focusing on particular cultural milieus where that discernment is occurring in new and unfamiliar forms: Hence the issues of 1975, *On Youth and the Future of the Church*, of 1977, *The Churches of Africa*, of 1979, *Christianity and China*, of 1981, *On Where the Church is now*, have each addressed a specific set of issues in highly particular cultural locations. The aim was and is to discern the nature of Christian faith in that locale and to discern the importance of that witness for the universal, ecumenical Church.

These first two sets of concerns might be said to have outlined more fully the inner plurality of Christian praxis and reflection. Two further kinds of question have attempted to understand the relationships of Christian self-understanding to other forms of understanding. Those other forms must include both the increasingly urgent issue of the relationship between Christianity and the other world religions: (hence the 1976 issue, *Christians and Moslems*, and the 1978 issue, *Buddhism and Christianity*). Forms of self-understanding alternative to Christian faith must also include the need to think anew the relationships between Christian self-understanding and certain modern and often culturally dominant secular forms of self-understanding. Hence, the issue of 1982, *The Challenge of Psychology to Christian Faith*, and the issue of 1983, *Cosmology and Theology*.

What unites these very different kinds of questions and concerns is the drive to discern the signs of the times. The signs are, in fact, many, different, and sometimes mutually exclusive. The process of discernment must be tentative yet risk-taking, pluralistic yet deliberate. The choice of the word 'discern' suggests this willingness (because this necessity) to grope towards understanding, to abandon imperialist theological claims for Cartesian-like certainty, to recognise that we live in history in all its pluralistic, unsettling, ambiguous, even *fascinans et tremendum* actuality. The very title 'Project X', suggests, on one reading, that 'X' is the known unknown question and answer sought in all heuristic thought. Project 'X' is, in one sense, an exercise in *docta ignorantia*. What the *esprit* of that project resists is all theological pretensions to perfect control or to utter certainty (through clear and distinct ideas). We grope to discern the many dimensions and questions of that pluralistic and ambiguous situation.

The issues addressed by the ten years of Project 'X' are by no means exhaustive of the questions which need addressing in our theological situation. And the individual responses given to the issues already addressed are themselves, in fact, pluralistic and sometimes mutually contradictory—as any reader of any single issue of Project 'X' soon discovers. Where then amidst this plurality of voices is a unifying chord to be heard? It is in the suggestion that what we need above all in our increasingly disturbing and challenging situation is the risk of attending to *all* the signs of the times, not merely those which fit our temperament or our society. It is in the risk of hearing one another once again through all the cacophany of sounds. It is in the risk of attending to the Gospel of Jesus Christ as our singular clue to the possibility of true theological discernment.

How, then, amidst what William James once named the 'buzzing, blooming confusion' of experience itself do theologians in our period attempt to discern so many signs, so many voices? Through their Christian faith in Jesus Christ as the singular, decisive disclosure of who God is, what history and nature may be construed to be, and who we might become. To insist that Project 'X' has remained a Christian theological attempt to respond to these many issues and questions is, of course, simply to insist that Project 'X' remains a part of *Concilium* itself. Project 'X' remains, as any reader will testify, a curious part of that larger enterprise. For the concerns of Project 'X' do not neatly fit in any of the earlier sections nor do they neatly fit with one another. And yet Project 'X' has remained, from its first issue in 1973 to the last in 1983, a deliberately theological attempt to discern the ever-changing signs of the time and to respond to those signs under the sign of the Gospel of Jesus Christ.

It is not, therefore, the diverse issues that have united the concerns of Project 'X'. But it is also not only the attempt to discern the signs of the times in the light of the Gospel of Jesus Christ. It is also the attempt to discern those signs theologically.

2. A SHARED METHOD? THE REVISED CORRELATIONAL METHOD

It is this last, most properly theological, demand which unites the ten issues of

Project 'X' with the rest of *Concilium*. In spite of a wide and growing plurality of particular models for theology, there does seem to be a shared general model for theological reflection in our period. In its simplest form, this model can be named a revised correlational model for theology. More exactly, theology in our period has many particular models for theology. The particularity of each is largely determined by the particular set of questions and discernments of our contemporary situation which demand theological response and the equally particular interpretations of certain symbols, doctrines, images, and narratives, etc., chosen from the Christian Gospel to respond to those questions. And yet, amidst the 'blooming, buzzing confusion' of this plurality of particular models for theology, there does seem to emerge in the theology of Project 'X', as of *Concilium* as a whole, a general, heuristic model for all theological reflection which informs the more particular models.

Let us, therefore, recall the most important characteristics of that general model. First, a definition: theology is the attempt to develop mutually critical correlations in both theory and praxis between an interpretation of the Christian tradition and an interpretation of the contemporary situation. In one sense, this now familiar 'revised correlational' model is simply a rendering explicit and deliberate of the fact which unites all forms of theology, viz., the fact that every Christian theology *is* interpretation of Christianity. Precisely as *interpretation* of the tradition, there can be no naïve claims to immediacy nor to certainty. There can and must be claims, however, to a genuine mediated and situated understanding of the tradition itself. As Christian interpreters of the Christian tradition, we recognise that the history of the effects of that tradition are present to and in all theologians both consciously and, more importantly, unconsciously. Theologians have the task, therefore, to render as explicit as possible an interpretation of the central Christian message for a concrete situation and to show why others should, in principle, agree with that interpretation.

As soon as any theologian interprets the tradition, she/he can also recognise that it is *we* ourselves who are doing the interpreting. It is, in sum, concrete human beings in concrete personal, social, cultural, political circumstances who are asking questions— some ancient, some unnervingly new—of the tradition. In so far as we are interpreting the Christian tradition seriously—i.e., theologically—we acknowledge its claim to truth, its claim to our full attention, its claim to challenge not only our present answers but even our present questions. In so far as *we* are *interpreting* that tradition seriously, we also recognise that we are not subject-less, context-less, history-less interpreters. We are no other than ourselves in these particular, concrete personal, social, cultural political circumstances. We attempt to grope our way to an understanding of those circumstances. We attempt to discern the signs of our times—the truly significant issues and places where the signs may be present.

Unlike Hegel, we do not believe that *we* possess an 'absolute knowledge' for this process of discernment of either our historical situation or the tradition. Like Hegel, and unlike the neo-Scholastics, we do believe that even reason has a history, that the 'not yet', the negative, is part of tradition and situation alike as well as all our discernments of each. We pursue not certainty but understanding. And we pursue that understanding with the knowledge that our interpretations, too, will prove inadequate, for *all* is interpretation.

The groping, tentative, even sometimes stumbling, character of the interpretations of both the tradition and the signs of the times in the issues of Project 'X' is not, therefore, a weakness but a strength.

It is, more exactly, the only strength available to us: the need to interpret the pluralistic and even ambiguous tradition for an ever-changing pluralistic and ambiguous situation, the need to give up the quest for an illusory a-historical certainty and live the quest for a situated understanding of the Christian Gospel in this place at this time.

The revised correlational model defined above is nothing other than the attempt to render explicit this inevitable process of properly theological interpretation. The model's only real claim is that it is not imposed upon the process of interpretation but is an accurate explication of the process of interpretation itself. To understand theology, therefore, as the attempt to develop mutually critical correlations in both theory and praxis between an interpretation of the Christian tradition and an interpretation of the contemporary situation is simply to render explicit the principal moments in contemporary theological interpretation. If the model succeeds it does provide a general heuristic model—no more, no less. That model, as heuristic and general, can guide the concrete programmes of concrete and particular differing theologies. The model can never *replace* those concrete, particular theologies any more than the general and abstract can ever replace the concrete.

To recognise, with A. N. Whitehead, the dangers of the 'fallacy of misplaced concreteness' is also to acknowledge, again with Whitehead, the value of the abstract. To abstract a general, heuristic model that in fact is shared by all contemporary theologians who have embraced a situated understanding and have abandoned the illusion of a context-less certainty is to aid all theologians to interpret and thereby to converse and argue over their differing interpretations. As John Courtney Murray justly observed, it takes a great deal of agreement in any community to allow for genuine disagreements. If we focus only on the disagreements we seldom if ever realise how much agreement there must be in order that we all know that, on this particular question or interpretation, we really do disagree.

If theology is to remain a communal discipline where all theologians can know where they differ and why they disagree, there must be sufficient agreement on the nature of the inquiry itself to allow those differences to become fruitful and those disagreements to be discussable by the whole theological community of inquiry. For this very reason, the ten issues of Project 'X' provide a useful test-case of the question of theological reflection today. For, as suggested above, there is *no* one question which unites these ten issues and there is no single answer on any of the particular questions addressed *within* each issue which remains unchallenged by other respondents within the same issue.

What, then, is a reader of all ten issues to think? Some may suggest that Project 'X' represents an excellent illustration of the 'chaos' of contemporary theology. Neo-Scholastics and all traditionalists and fundamentalists would surely make this charge before returning to their untroubled and a-historical fortresses. Others may suggest that Project 'X' demonstrates an unintended example of that kind of 'lazy pluralism' which simply cloaks real differences by blessing all difference, the kind of pluralism which is driven not by the pursuit of situated understanding but by an unconscious indifference to truth and argument, a kind of pluralism which quickly degenerates into a 'repressive tolerance' (Marcuse).

My suggestion throughout these reflections is that neither chaos nor 'repressive tolerance' adequately expresses the kind of pluralistic theological reflection represented by *Concilium* as a whole and expressed, in a particularly intense form, in the ten issues of Project 'X'. My suggestion is, rather, that any careful reader of those ten issues can observe that, sometimes through differences and sometimes in spite of them, the different theological proposals suggest that a shared general model of theological reflection is also present—and present as shared. There is a sufficiently shared element to allow any reader to know that theology is a discipline with communal, i.e., shared, disciplinary ideals. For every theological author in every issue, in fact, engages in the kind of contemporary situated theological interpretation outlined above.

Indeed, the general revised correlational model which renders explicit that kind of contemporary theological interpretation is also present throughout the theological articles in each issue. Each theologian, precisely by abandoning pretensions to a-historical certainty and by embracing situated interpretation as understanding, works implicitly or explicitly with a revised correlational model. This means that, as a contemporary theologian, every theologian is a concretely situated interpreter of the tradition for a concrete situation. Every theologian, precisely as interpreter, must interpret the tradition for and in a concrete situation. In so far as they do that they find themselves interpreting both the tradition *and* the contemporary situation. They interpret the situation, as Christian theologians, by attempting to provide Christian construals of that situation under the rubric of 'discerning the signs of the times'. Those discernments, in turn, lead them to interpret the tradition itself anew. They interpret the tradition both to retrieve often forgotten, even repressed disclosive and transformative aspects of tradition (e.g., the mystico-political symbols of liberation, emancipation and redemption). They also interpret the tradition not only with a hermeneutics of retrieval but also of critique and suspicion: by recognising, for example, the privatising elements in the tradition, by criticising (as in the issue on cosmology) the fatal silence on nature in much Western, including contemporary, theology, by rendering explicit repressed systematic distortions in the tradition (sexism, racism, classism, anti-Semitism, élitism, ect.).

In so far as theologians engage in hermeneutics of both retrieval and critique-suspicion of *both* the tradition and the situation, they also implicitly correlate the results of all these interpretations. Those correlations will inevitably prove to be, moreover, correlations in both praxis and theory. The correlations will ordinarily prove 'mutually critical'—a phrase introduced to remind theologians that prior to the actual analysis there is no way of predicting what concrete kind of correlation is needed in this particular instance. In some cases, here will be a *confrontation* between the Christian tradition and the contemporary situation. In other cases, mutually critical *analogies* (as similarities-in-difference) may prove what is needed. In rarer cases, an effective *identity* of meaning may obtain.

In sum, a revised correlational method is simply a rendering explicit of what happens in every concretely situated theological act of interpretation. The revisionary character of the present model is revisionary by spelling out more explicitly three factors which earlier 'liberal' models of correlation tended to ignore. First, 'correlation' is a logical category which suggests a whole spectrum of possible responses: either identity (*no* difference) or analogy (similarities-in-difference) or even confrontation (mutually exclusive difference). Unlike some earlier liberal models of correlation there is no built-in 'prejudice' towards harmonisation in the contemporary correlational model. Second, this same principle is further clarified by the phrase 'mutually critical'. Here again, it is not the case as in some earlier formulations of a correlational model (e.g., Paul Tillich's) that there are 'questions' from one 'source' (the situation) and answers from another (the tradition). Rather, in every concrete case of theological interpretation there is need to allow for the kind of interaction that occurs in all true interpretation as genuine conversation. The need for real interaction between text and interpreter and thereby between tradition and situation is emphasised by the phrase 'mutually critical'. Third, the additional phrase 'in theory and in praxis' is also intended to remind concretely situated interpreters that every act of theological interpretation is concretely situated, that every correlation in theory is also a correlation in praxis. Praxis, too, should be rendered as explicit (in social, cultural and political terms) as possible in any attempt at genuine theological correlation.

To summarise: the revised method of correlation, thus interpreted, is simply meant to explicate the shared and thereby communal character of all truly contemporary theological interpretation. In as much as that method does its task of explication well, it aids the conversation which is the community of inquiry called theology. There exists sufficient agreement on what the contemporary theologian is doing when she/he is providing a situated theological interpretation of the tradition to ensure that disagreements will prove genuine disagreements within a real community of disciplined inquiry. The revised correlational method always remains only a general heuristic method to guide but never to replace the results of any concrete theological interpretation of the meaning and truth of a concrete symbol in a concrete situation. The general method guides as helpful abstractions always do. Every method that has not fallen into the temptation to become one more 'methodologism' remains a helpful and necessary abstraction. Methodologism is merely the latest outburst of the quest for a-historical certainty and the most recent expression of the fallacy of misplaced concreteness.

The revised correlational method is a method implicitly and sometimes explicitly employed in all contemporary, situated theology-as-interpretation. That method would become a methodologism only if it moved past its heuristic status and tried to replace any concrete theological interpretation. Yet recalling that method of correlation helps the entire theological community (or any reader of the ten issues of Project 'X' alone) to allow for a responsible pluralism, i.e., an arguing and often conflictual set of sometimes complementary differences, sometimes mutually exclusive disagreements within a shared context of some basic heuristic methodical agreements.

The general and abstract, the methodical, heuristically guide: they do not rule. Only the concrete rules—and the concrete is always a particular interpretation of a particular symbol for a particular situation. Some concluding and brief reflections of some of those particularities of content, therefore, may also aid our present reflections on the strange enterprise named Project 'X'.

3. PROSPECTIVE: THE PRIORITY OF THE FUTURE

For the Christian consciousness, origin is not end. And even 'end' is not a strict *telos* but finally an *adventum*: the genuinely new as threat and promise from God, the genuinely new in the situation we are called to discern, even the new in the tradition we are called to retrieve anew. Any attempt to suggest future reality from a Christian theological perspective, therefore, is not a prediction based on the origin of an already existing form—even so sprawling, plural and tentative a form as the several kinds of discernment represented in the ten issues of Project 'X'. It is sometimes observed with a quiet despair bordering on fatalism—even in theological circles, indeed even in progressive theological circles—that even the future is not what it used to be.

But the fact is it never was. For the Christian revolution of consciousness is a revolution which cannot stop and cannot presume to know with certainty either the future or the present or, as we saw above, even the past. The presentness of the past is present for the Christian consciousness as the presence of memories—subversive memories ever in need of retrieval to unleash their power anew. The presentness of the present is present through the ever-shifting moments of attention, discernment, interest in ever-new questions, constantly emerging new signs to discern and new demands for action and thought alike. The presentness of the future is present as *adventum* through the promises and threats of the Christian Gospel where that future Reign of God proclaimed by Jesus enters history ever anew to upset all calculations and where the always/already/not yet event of Jesus Christ keeps coming as *adventum* in ever-new forms. That event unleashes new demands for fresh interpretations and concrete actions in a situation where the future must have priority for the Christian consciousness.

Any 'prospective', therefore, for the kind of theological concerns and methods represented by Project 'X' thus far, can at best provide some 'hints and guesses' for the kind of theological work needed in the future. A retrospective, in and of itself, is not a prospective. Yet this much does seem suggested by this brief retrospective: the pluralism within Christian theology will increase and the demands of facing massive global suffering and the demands of facing the serious dialogue among the religions will also increase within Christian theological consciousness. The past suggests that the different kinds of difficult questions released in all theology by the kinds of concerns expressed in the different issues of Project 'X' will come anew in the future in yet more pointed and intense forms. If these questions are to come anew to be asked by a theological *community*, then something like the revised correlational method suggested above will need further revisions and demand further reflection and support.

We are, as a Christian theological community, just beginning to find ways to articulate the enrichments in our own inner-Christian ecumenical and thereby pluralistic reality. We are just beginning to formulate properly theological hermeneutics which can both retrieve the subversive memories of the tradition as well as criticise and suspect the actualities of error and systemic distortion in the tradition and situation alike. We are just beginning to find ways to allow the concrete personal, social, cultural and political contexts which impinge upon all our work to enter fully into theological reflection itself. We are just beginning to allow the mystico-political reality of Christian faith to enter into a dialogue serious enough to allow for mutual transformation with the other classic religions and the classic secular, scientific, humanistic and post-humanistic world-views. We are just beginning. We are, by any reasonable account, not-yet there.

As the entry of the crucial adverb 'not-yet' indicates, the sense of the priority of the future over both the present and the past must come to dominate all Christian theological reflection. But that is as it should be: for it is clearly not the time for Project 'X' or *Concilium* or the wider theological community to rest in the present or bask in a sense of false self-congratulations for the past. The sense of all that is not-yet is too strong to allow for any such premature and finally immature closure. For the signs of the times are once again upon us. And those signs are signs of the priority of the future—possibilities and promises like a genuine religious pluralism in an emerging global community we have not yet dared to imagine; threats like nuclear holocaust and ecological disaster we have not presumed to face; above all, the full actuality of the always/already/not yet *adventum* of Jesus Christ in our midst.

Origin is not end. Retrospective is not prospective. To propose that what we should most expect is the unexpected is not Utopian but cold realism. That much, at least, the honest, troubled strivings expressed in the various discernments of the signs of the times in Project 'X' over the last ten years can teach us. For 'X' remains the unknown. We find ourselves open to the future as the unknown, the unexpected with neither certainty nor security but with that *docta ignorantia* granted us by the always/already/not yet event of Jesus Christ.

DAVID TRACY
(co-editor of Project 'X' since 1980 with Professor Giuseppe Alberigo)

Peter Huizing and Knut Walf

Concilium's Programme for the Section on Church Law

Part I (by Peter Huizing)

THE FIRST issue on Church Law in 1965 presented the programme envisaged for this section within the framework of a theological journal as aiming at 'detheologising Canon Law' and 'dejuridicising theology' (p. 4). Both the explanation of this programme and the way it was subsequently worked out emphasised the essential link between faith and Church law, between theology and canon law, while at the same time pointing to the danger which threatens both equally. The danger is that in every community the balance between historically developed and therefore changeable structures on the one hand, and the concept, or, if preferred, the ideal of people living together, is constantly threatened *and* constantly disturbed. The danger is that people identify so much with these historical structures that they idealise these structures and see them as the only possible embodiment of the 'ideal'. This obviously means that constantly less idealistic and more self-interested motives are accepted as realistic. Thus the ideal and the structures get all so ossified that any further attempt to reach the ideal by a more open development of the structures is not only hampered but rejected in principle. This has the tragic consequence that the only way in which development can be pursued is by violence, and this violence will turn against both the ideal and the structures in their ossified state.

In the Christian community the danger lies in structures, particularly the juridical ones, which have sprung up in the course of history, being presented as a matter of 'faith' or as the only way of expressing the faith. In other words, these structures are being 'theologised'. But the result of this is that the object of the faith and theology is reduced to the juridical structures which happen to exist, so that faith and theology are being 'juridicised'. Here we have simply two aspects of the same process.

The programme of 1965 already mentioned a few instances of what was happening: the ways in which the seven sacraments developed in history were put forward as 'instituted by Christ'; the present Western structure of the appointment and function of bishops was 'theologised' as 'participation in the pastoral function of the pope'. There are obviously hundreds of other examples which would illustrate the process. To mention only a few: the various powers claimed by the papacy in the course of the centuries have been 'theologised' as the pope's *vicaria potestas*; structures for which no

37

proof can be found in the Scriptures have been 'theologised' as 'based on Christ's example'; the rejection of any judicial check on the unjust exercise of authority has been 'theologised' as a necessary consequence of the *sacra potestas* of the hierarchy; the indissolubility of the sacramental and consummated marriage has been theologised by reference to the 'one flesh' (Matt. 19:5f.), and so on.

People's attachment to their faith will obviously spill over on to the concrete ways in which they experience this faith. So they may find a certain tentative and pious way of theologising these ways helpful. There is no justification for disturbing them in this area unnecessarily. But this 'theologising' of historical structures should be critically dealt with whenever and in so far as such structures upset people in the practice and joy of their faith; discriminate between people and groups, deprive people of their rights or leave them in this state; reduce people to a state of nonage or leave them there; when power is 'theologised' for the sake of more power; when people are alienated from their own culture, and, in short, whenever and in so far as Church law no longer hangs on the first commandment and the second, on an equal level with it, on which 'the whole Law and the prophets hang' (Matt. 22:40); in other words, when it hampers and obstructs the Spirit of Jesus. This is surely the deepest root of the Catholic tradition—the ultimate canonically valid criterion by which to judge the canonical structures of the Church. According to the programme of 1965 the contribution of canon law to *Concilium* must follow the lines indicated by Vatican II, and therefore be 'catholic', which means it must profess the belief in Christ as meant for all peoples and cultures as well as for each individual human person. It must therefore be both 'pastoral' and 'ecumenical', i.e., aiming at locally and individually adapted pastoral care throughout the whole Catholic community as well as at the growth of all Christians towards a universal communion. This implies that the inherent critical function with regard to the existing law, including its presuppositions based on faith or theology, is of the essence of a canonist's task and responsibility—something of which the post-conciliar generation of canon lawyers has become more fully aware.

The first issue emphasised that the believing Church exists as a communion of sisters and brothers and that this communion demands *canonical structures to enable them to act collegially* at every level, from the episcopal college to the parish community. It has rightly been pointed out that the wholly specific nature of the community based on Jesus—*communio*—where all are brothers and sisters and nobody must be called master or father or teacher (Matt. 23:8f.) and where all leadership remains simply being sent by the Lord (John 17:18; 20:21-23; Matt. 28:18-20), demands wholly specific structures of a truly collegial nature. This demand is in no way met by structures which only secure and emphasise the right of leaders to take decisions exclusively as their privilege, where everybody else is reduced to 'purely consultative' status. This does not usually happen in the case of true leaders.

The issue on *Religious Freedom* (1966) dealt with the consequences of the relevant conciliar Declaration on the co-operation of all Christian churches, the relation with non-Christian religions, the dialogue with those who do not believe in God, the missions, and freedom of opinion within the Catholic Church.

Concerning the relationship between faith and Church law, and between theology and the science of canon law, the programme of 1965 implied that the truths of the faith are *postulates* which that law has to accept, but become unreal ideological statements if put forward as self-substantiating dogmatic and ontological facts of the faith, since, in actual fact, no concrete canonical formulation can do full justice to any single dogmatic postulate. Thus the proclamation of the message and the celebration of the sacraments are bound to be central to Church law: it *must* support the living local community and the religious maturity of the members of the Church; it *must* be of service to the mission of lay people in the world, etc. But canon law does not do all this automatically. For too long canon law seemed to consider it a matter of 'faith' or 'piety' to propose as an apodictic matter of faith that all sectors of Church law achieved all this by themselves on the basis of the wisdom of the legislators or the guidance of the Holy Spirit. Any criticism of canon law came practically exclusively from non-Catholic canonist scholars. Among Catholics it remained practically simply a matter of improving legal and systematic technicalities. This, too, was an effect of the aprioristic nature of the study and practice of canon law which was itself the result of the petrifying theologisation of canon law.

One of the failings of canon law which is often criticised is that it lacks a sense of reality, or of common sense. This, too, was vented several times in *Concilium* (see P. Shannon 'The Code of Canon Law, 1918-1967'; P. Boyle 'Renewal and Resolutions of the Canon Law Society of America', 1967, pp. 26ff. and 36ff.; P. Huizing 'The Indissolubility of Marriage and Church Order', 1968, p. 25ff.; A. Greeley 'Canon Law and Society', 1969, pp. 67ff.).

The Programme of 1965 insisted that on-going attention should be paid to the real functioning of Church law. Actually, this field has hardly been broken up. In practice Church leaders and canonists have no idea what becomes of whole pieces of canon law in very large regions. This applies also to the so-called developed provinces of the Church. Thus the vast differences which exist in the way neighbouring dioceses deal with marital processes cannot be attributed to such vast differences in marital practice and experience but rather to the various ways in which the responsible Church authorities see their task since some of them occasionally show little appreciation of genuine human need and distress. Often, too, pastoral necessity leads to local pastoral measures which are not publicised for understandable reasons but which imperceptibly make the 'official' legal administration meaningless. Occasionally one even meets a deliberate ignoring of reality, based on the conviction that in any case this reality can in no way affect the law which is based on principles.

Following the image of the Church as presented by Vatican II and particularly the Constitution on the Church in the World of Today, *Gaudium et Spes*, described as 'the Church turning towards the world', the study of Church law has the task of investigating the *structures of the Church's presence in the world* (1970) in the light of their efficacy. It is precisely these structures which, for a large part called forth by historical circumstances and therefore relative, should therefore maintain a fair degree of adaptability. This point is not primarily a matter of the diplomatic relations and activities of the Holy See, since these are there to serve the more pastorally effective presence of the local churches among their own people. The principles and concrete expressions of the Church's presence in the world of today no longer fit into the scheme of Church and State seen each as a 'perfect society' in its own right, which the old textbooks on 'public Church law' interpreted as a matter of the relations between the papacy and sovereign governments. How inadequate these structures had become in modern society became apparent from, among other things, *the protest movement within the Catholic Church* (1971). This movement sprang up after the surprisingly open-minded and truly collegial event of Vatican II, and was called forth by the continuing vertical structuring of Church government, linked with a policy which neutralised any more inspired attempts. Unfortunately, this active protest movement petered out gradually and led to a passive and silent but massive turning away from a Church with that kind of structures.

As a complicated example of an ideologically loaded sector of ecclesiastical structures we might look at the on-going debate, not so much about the celibacy of priests as such, but rather about *canon law linking this celibacy with the office of priesthood* (1972). Although this debate revealed profound differences between one continent and another, it also showed that a considerable majority of those interviewed were very critical about this coupling of the two subjects by canon law.

The investigation of *the Church's legislation concerning the contract, annulment and dissolution of marriage* (1973), where the key issue was whether present canon law reflects the one and only accurate interpretation of marital fidelity according to the Gospel for members of the Church, also showed in any case that this section of Church law, too, has no real effect on this fidelity as it is experienced by these members, since the percentage of civil divorce in their case is practically the same as that among other groups of the population. There, too, one observes a rather general and often pronounced aversion to the formal, juridical and celibate approach to such momentous crises in life as the disruption of a marriage implies in most, if not all, cases.

The tension between traditional ways of life, structures and relationships on the one hand, and the urge towards being more personally bound up with a more communal experience of the Gospel on the other, has also profoundly affected *the religious life* (1974) which is going through a severe crisis in very wide areas. Within the traditional structures of orders, congregations, communities and secular associations there is a radical shift going on in the understanding and practice of canonical impositions regarding the vows of obedience, poverty and celibacy, and in the way one understands one's own personal mission. The factual data so far provide no more than rather hesitant pointers to the future. It would appear that the new trends towards new ways of leading the religious life are mainly developing away from the existing canonical stuctures.

The *penal law of the Church* (1975) also raises the question whether it does not drag along with it antiquated remnants of ages past, even more so than other sectors of Church law. Apart from people who are employed by the Church and owe it their livelihood, coercive ecclesiastical sanctions are no longer operative in most countries. Where extra-ecclesiastical social sanctions such as the threat of being sacked from non-ecclesial posts or losing one's reputation would still be possible, most right-minded people resent this as socially unacceptable and as contradicting the principle of religious freedom which rejects any social duress based on religious motivation. This does not alter the fact that a Church community owes it to itself and its identity—therefore to its Lord—to be responsible for its own character and mission and to protect these against threats and interferences, including those which come from within. This, in turn, may entail measures taken against particular persons such as depriving them of some function or the right to take part in liturgical celebrations of the Church. If necessary, such measures could also be aimed at the political or other social behaviour of Church members if such behaviour seriously threatened or interfered with the true identity of the community. One even wonders whether, particularly today, we do not need such measures far more than the illusory punishments for violence directed at popes and other members of the clergy, or at abortion, heresy and suchlike. Such a 'turning towards the world' on the part of Church law in connection with canonical sanctions would probably do the Church more good today than unreal and ineffectual measures taken within the ecclesiastical set-up.

The issue on *Believing by Order?* (1976) raises one of the most serious problems in the present crisis about the credibility of the Catholic Church, particularly its *magisterium*. The constantly returning one-sided emphasis on the formal, juridical legitimation of the college of bishops as successors to the apostles and therefore as the exclusive representatives of the *magisterium* threatens to reduce the faith of the Church community to mere docility, while this *magisterium* is, or in any case should be, rightly vested in the whole community which believes and trusts that it bears genuine witness to the truth of the Gospel on which the Church's life is based. This reinforces the impression that Catholics only believe what they are told by the hierarchy to such a degree that it obscures the credibility of the Gospel itself in Catholic belief. Without *magisterium* the Church becomes rudderless, but without the Church the *magisterium* runs into sterile isolation. The *magisterium* has no power to impose or prescribe faith. It can only function within the living community of the faith and is rooted in the faith of the whole body. 'Catholics do not believe in Christ because their hierarchy tells them so but accept the authority of the hierarchy because they believe in the mission with which Christ entrusted them.'

The issue on *The Function of the Ecclesiastical Judge* (1977) deals with the role of the administration of justice in the Church. The Church tribunals are the oldest in the legal tradition of the West. In the middle ages their judgments led to the establishment of humane principles of law, based on the dignity of the human person, and these principles are still the foundation of civil law. Today these tribunals take decisions which are practically nowhere accepted in civil law. Sacramental life is wrapped up in judicial features: admonitions, forgiveness, petition and exhortation—all are linked with the administration of the law. How should the ecclesiastical judge see his function in the light of the Gospel and of human wisdom?

Public statements and information about a lawsuit occur rarely. In general the faithful are little impressed by the publication of some judgment, e.g., in a book written about it. Since the Council experience has shown that secrecy in the administration of justice and confidentiality of judicial deeds are not always a blessing. There are injustices in the Church, such as when wrongdoers are brought to court but are let off because they have power or influence or can pull strings with friends. There must be a judicial protection of rights. 'Without legal restitution rights are futile in the Church.' 'Today honesty in the Church demands that any member of the faithful can appeal to a judicial office in the Church, which guarantees justice in a straightforward and open manner.' Thus, in the aftermath of *Humanae Vitae*, hundreds of men and women were sacked from their educational posts. This showed, among other things, that although the encyclical raised fierce controversy among moral theologians, there was no protection for those who differed from the established line and for basic rights. It also revealed the vast and disturbing lack of adaptability in Church law. The Church had no means whatsoever of coping with a massive difference of opinion apart from an enforced compromise or excommunication. The result was an alienation from the Church of alarming proportions. The principal cause of this was not the actual difference of opinion but rather the lack of trust in the Church, which meant specifically the Church authorities. In this crisis judgments were made arbitrarily, without any definite norms and without any chance of appealing to impartial bodies.

If it is now possible to reconcile the official teaching of the Church with the practical imperatives of a committed and living faith, it is only because this reconciliation was forced by those who spoke out in the anguish of their conscience and were despised by the Church, but who solved the problem for millions who kept quiet.

Would this stage lead to a regime marked by rehabilitation and understanding? Because of particular ecclesiastical procedures people are branded as unfit. They are subjected to punitive measures without an opportunity to defend themselves or to explain their motives to an impartial party while the issue as such, based on natural law, was debatable.

The period after the Council was marked by conflicts of a theological and institutional nature. A conflict is never abstract, never a merely intellectual difference of opinion. It is a clash of personalities, often leading to alienation and doing permanent damage. In the Church one person confronts another in a most profound crisis of identity because both believe that the Church is in truth a communion of grace, understanding, reconciliation and justice. An appeal to Rome is a poor substitute for an impartial party. Moreover, if there is a conflict of roles, should the judge settle a quarrel or serve the interests of the Church? Can these roles be kept separate and what would such a separation imply? In the Church justice and the administration of justice are indeed problematic. A revision of canon law cannot simply ignore this. In its general behaviour the Church still remains a paternalistic institution which dispenses justice at its own discretion. The authors of the issue under discussion say that they wrote 'in the belief that, from now on, the Church can take the initiative in becoming a community where true justice reigns as a carefully fostered and procedurally attainable ideal'.

It is dangerous to take external quiet as a yardstick by which to measure justice. These days, so sensitive to this matter of justice, people expect of the Church that it will contribute to an improvement in judicial functions in order to ensure justice for all.

The issue on *Church Finance* (1978) aimed at providing information about the present situation of the finances of the Church and the problems which arise from its financial structures. Today the administration of Church property should no longer rely on capitalist methods of investing large capital sums for long periods but on a new awareness of all the faithful that they share a common responsibility for the welfare of all as well as for the maintenance of the various services in the Church, including that of the administration. This requires the formation of a new collective opinion.

For some ten years Church contributions to development aid for mainly charitable purposes have been integrated in political activity in order to create an informed public opinion, particularly in industrialised countries. Is there a chance that the 'old churches', recognising the right to self-determination of the 'new churches', will contribute to fairer relations between the nations and a new just international legal order? Are the churches still (again?) the 'stewards of the poor'?

All this also demands a re-orientation of the Petrine office: instead of an administrative and controlling authority it should rather become a spiritual and moral centre.

Moreover, it is likely that the expertise required for financial administration and its switch-over to a more ecclesial direction in the way mentioned above, will be found among experienced layfolk rather than among the clergy.

Part II (by Knut Walf)

Various proposals were made to the section on Church Order at the General Assembly of 1979 and at subsequent meetings. These proposals or subjects fitted into a tradition which developed in the course of the years on the one hand, but, on the other, were inspired by some disturbing information about the final stage of the new codification of canon law. It is somehow in the tradition of this section of *Concilium* to deal with the relationship between the local churches and the Church at large as well as with the structural problems these local churches have to face. In other words, the core of this section is still the vast ecclesiological issue of Vatican II: the collegiality which should shape the relations between the pope and the bishops.

For the local churches and the protection or creation of their identity, the question of how and through whose influence their bishops are selected, nominated and appointed constitutes an urgent problem (*Local Church and Episcopal Election*) 1980. The collegiality which governs or should govern the relations between pope and bishops as among all the bishops of the Church at large finds its most important expression in the ecumenical council. Among the reports we obtained about the work of the commission charged with framing the new Code the most disturbing element was that the ecumenical council was upstaged with regard to its significance and its traditional role in the context of this new Code.

Through a leak it became publicly known that a 1976 draft of an ecclesiastical constitution only dealt with the ecumenical council after the episcopal synod, the college of cardinals and other 'institutions' (Roman Curia?). It was even more surprising to find that the 1980 draft of the Code did not even mention the ecumenical council at all but only the episcopal synod, the college of cardinals and the Roman Curia.

We therefore deemed it necessary to stress the ecclesiological importance of the council. At the same time we wanted to make it clear that the very name of our periodical impelled us to sound the alarm when we noticed that the ecumenical council was at risk as an institution ('The Ecumenical Council in the Church Constitution', 1983).

In 1982 we dealt with a topic which, at first sight, has nothing to do with the tension between local churches and the universal Church: *May Church Ministers be Politicians?*. But when we look a little more closely at this issue it becomes clear that it has created a conflict between a number of local churches and Rome. One has only to think of the political activities in which priests, both secular and regular, are involved as the inevitable consequence of liberation theology. And in many North-Atlantic countries a vast number of priests have to face the possibility of an atomic holocaust. In the 1982 issue of *Concilium* we have dealt with the actuality of this subject, even more actual now since the 1983 Code shows such a negative attitude towards the political activity of secular or regular members of the clergy.

We naturally saw it also as our task to draw attention at the right time to the trends and main features of the new canon law and to provide such information as was available at the time of writing. But this was rather difficult, since it raised two questions: When was the right time? and: How could we give responsible information about a legal project which we knew as little about as the rest of the interested public? When in 1981 we got hold of the 1980 draft Code—through another (deliberate?) leak—we decided to risk it. But since there was still uncertaintly about so many things we cautiously entitled it: *The Revised Code of Canon Law: A Missed Opportunity*. As we saw later, we chose the right moment. For, towards the end of 1982 the public was rather surprisingly informed that the Code was to be promulgated in January 1983, and the text was only published in the beginning of February. This meant that for many commentators in periodicals and other publications *Concilium* had provided them with the relevant information. This meant, in turn, that these commentators took over much of the views and considerations from the authors who contributed to our issue. It is therefore fair to say that *Concilium* influenced the mainly critical reception of the Code.

If we look at the view of Church organisation as we have put it in this article as well as in the trend and choice of topics dealt with in *Concilium* we should understand that this sector of *Concilium* will, for a short or longer term, be involved in taking a critical look at the way this new Code is received in the Church. But since, in our opinion, the new Code presents a one-sided view of the institutional Church future issues will tackle topics and issues which are not determined just in terms of this Code.

When we look into a future which is unclear and therefore perhaps rather frightening, for the Church and its theology also, then we see the rather rough outline of the main issues on which this sector will have to concentrate.

The first point has already been mentioned: *Concilium* must keep up its critical comments on the way the new Code is received. It would be wrong if we treated the expected discussions and controversies about the content and aims of this new, yet mainly traditional, law on the basis of another concept of Church organisation. *Concilium*, far from ignoring the new Code, should participate in this debate since at present it is a matter of supporting the few positive points presented in the new Code while developing others, such as the position of the laity, and particularly the place and function of women, We also have in mind new elements in marriage law or legal procedure (administrative jurisdiction).

The second point is that we shall have to base our views on the point that it is not the law which determines life but rather that life influences, changes and shapes the law: *ius sequitur vitam*. We are convinced that, in view of the profound changes in society, the Church, too, will have to change. Its structures and laws strike many of its members as something alien and incomprehensible and are no longer plausible. *Concilium* will therefore have to make the law come face to face with the living reality, which really means with the reality of the law itself, since ultimately only the life of actual people is real. If *Concilium* also fosters the reconsideration of old values which might vanish into oblivion, this is not merely for the sake of completeness. Canon lawyers know full well that their on the whole very conservative discipline contains values in its tradition which may help to provide a solution for modern issues.

The third main point is that in the end Western church law must constantly be checked by comparison with other legal systems and concepts. More than ever before we want to take up impulses that reach us from the system of Anglo-American law. We will venture into wholly new territory when we investigate more thoroughly what countries of the Third World offer today in the way of new forms of community life in the Church, and what is being tried out in so many basic communities.

If we want to put our programme for the future in one sentence we would say that *Concilium* wants to break through the narrow limits of codified Church law and keep a critical eye on whatever new regulations may arise within the Church.

Translated by Theo Westow

Hans Küng

Twenty Years of Ecumenical Theology—What For?

IN THE beginning was the Council—the Council no one thought possible until John XXIII, towering above all his predecessors and successors this century in both humanity and Christianity, summoned the Second Vatican Council. His programme was, instead of counter-Reformation, the re-union of divided Christians and churches by means of reform of his own Church. It was without question an epoch-making turning-point in the Catholic Church's relationship to all other churches, an opportunity for the complete refashioning of Catholic ecumenism. This is what *Concilium* wanted to take into account.

1. *CONCILIUM* AS A SEQUEL TO THE COUNCIL

One thing was clear to those who started *Concilium*: a relapse into the age before Vatican II should and must no longer exist for Catholic theology and for the Catholic Church, a relapse into an age when one self-righteously shielded one's own church from criticism and was only aware of the worst side of the other, when ignorance of, aversion to and neglect of the common Christian heritage was dominant and polemic and conflict were triumphant on both sides in the theological and social fields.

No, the aim was to build on Vatican II and to move forward. This Council recognised the Catholic share in blame for schism and the necessity of continual reform; asked other Christians for forgiveness; and called for a renewal of the Church's life and teaching in keeping with the Gospel of Jesus Christ. This Council addressed other Christians no longer simply as individuals but as communities, and not just as any kind of community but as ecclesial communities or churches. This Council demanded an ecumenical attitude of the whole Church: prayer and inner conversion by everyone, getting to know the other side and trying to understand them through dialogue, recognising the good in them and learning from them. The faith, the love, and the baptism of other Christians was recognised and the need was seen for theology and Church history to be conducted in an ecumenical spirit.

This Council also came out in favour of practical co-operation with other Christians throughout the entire social field. It wanted joint prayer. It encouraged increased sharing in worship, particularly in the liturgy of the Word. It initiated dialogue between theologians at the same level: non-Catholic observers at the Council, Catholic observers at the World Council of Churches. Numerous dialogues got under way.

All this is laid down in the Council's decree on ecumenism and applies both to the churches of the Reformation and to the Orthodox churches of the East. But with regard to the latter the Council went considerably further, as can be seen from the decree on the Eastern Catholic churches in communion with Rome. Previously these were often regarded as a venerable and fundamentally obsolete appendage of the real or Latin Church—the Eastern rites—while they had become an increasing obstacle to unity between the Latin Church and the Orthodox churches separated from Rome, particularly because they themselves had to some extent become strongly influenced by Latin and Roman models in their rites and spirituality. This decree on the Eastern churches in communion with Rome is important for the Catholic Church's relationship with Orthodoxy in general. Among the points it makes are:

> The variety of the different churches does not damage but rather strengthens unity. The churches of the East have the same rights as those of the West. They have the right and the duty to cherish their own liturgy, canon law and spirituality and in certain circumstances to restore these.

> The ancient rights and privileges of the Eastern Patriarchs are to be restored. In particular, to them falls the appointment of bishops. Where they share the same territory they should co-operate.

> The Catholic Eastern churches should pray and work for the unity of the Church. Orthodox Christians who become Catholic are not required to be re-baptised, nor is there any demand for the re-ordination of ordained Orthodox priests. Orthodox Christians can, if they wish, receive the sacraments in Catholic churches, and in reverse Catholics can receive the sacraments in Orthodox churches provided no Catholic priest is available. Mixed marriages between Catholics and Orthodox are valid even if they are not solemnised in a Catholic Church. Sharing of churches is allowed. . . .

Why could Vatican II not go as far with regard to the churches of the Reformation? With this question we reach the neuralgic point of the ecumenical debate at this Council. Questions of this kind had to some extent remained reserved for higher authority. But the progressive majority at the Council accepted at the time that many of these questions would, with the help of the Secretariat for Promoting Christian Unity that had been established, obviously be solved after the Council so as to reach a developing understanding both with the churches of the East and with the churches of the Reformation. This was the starting-point for *Concilium* and particularly its section on ecumenism. An advisory editorial committee was formed from the best-known Catholic ecumenists, joined later by leading Orthodox and Protestant theologians. The secretary and later joint editor of the section was Walter Kasper, originally my assistant at Tübingen but subsequently professor of dogmatic theology first at Münster and then at Tübingen: our co-operation was always free of friction and constructive. When Kasper left in 1978 the Tübingen Protestant theologian Jürgen Moltmann was chosen to succeed him by the central board of editorial directors, an appointment that underlined the section's ecumenical character.

A presupposition in the work of this section was that today Christian theology had in general to be ecumenical theology, concerned with the anxieties, wishes and hopes of the Christian *oikoumene*, of the whole Christian world. In fact all the issues of the journal have been meant to be inspired, informed and directed by this aim, and it can be said that the issues dealing with exegesis, dogma and moral theology, with Church history, canon law and pastoral theology are also always planned and written in the spirit of ecumenical understanding.

2. NEURALGIC POINTS

The particular aim of the issue devoted to ecumenism was to bring the neuralgic points of ecumenical understanding into the field of view: theological questions that usually have practical consequences and practical questions that usually cannot be solved without a good theological foundation. In this way, in *Concilium*, theology, which in the past had only too often piled up enormous road-blocks in the way of Christian unity, set to work to build solid and often daring bridges towards other Christians.

The first ecumenism issue appeared in 1965, the year the Council came to an end. It began with problems that had played an important role at the Council but had not yet been sufficiently thoroughly discussed in theology and in the Church: whether missionary activity was an obstacle or a stimulus to ecumenism; *communicatio in sacris* with Eastern Christians separated from Rome in the light of history; the charismatic structure of the Church; the ecclesial reality of the other churches; the Church under the word of God; and the function of the World Council of Churches.

While with one exception all the contributors to the first issue were Catholics, the second issue (1966), entitled *Other Christian Churches—do we know them?*, showed that in the section on ecumenism the theologians of other churches should be able to make important statements on an equal footing, while we were of course concerned that *Concilium* as a whole should not deny its Catholic origin. What did Luther really want? What would Calvin say to present-day Catholics? These questions were answered by Catholic and Protestant contributors. The ecumenical significance of Karl Barth and of Rudolf Bultmann was presented by Catholic theologians, while Orthodox theologians handled Orthodoxy's fundamental demands with regard to the Catholic Church. An Anglican presented the witness of the Anglican Communion and a Methodist that of the American Free Churches, with a response by a Catholic.

In this way we quickly found our own style in the section on ecumenism: acting as a forum for the different theologies of the different churches, open to everyone who was concerned not just to repeat what was already known but to use their scholarship to provide constructive help. Thus, in the 1967 issue, devoted to *The Debate on the Sacraments*, Joseph Ratzinger together with the Dutch Catholic theologians Piet Schoonenberg and Wim Boelens offered a response to the questions of Protestant and Orthodox eucharistic theology raised by Renzo Bertalot and John Meyendorff. Ought not the international and inter-denominational community of theologians to function in this way, communicating without domination, has it not functioned in this way, and could it not function again in this way? Along with this there was from the start no attempt to duck the disputed and 'dangerous' questions, such as divorce and remarriage in the Eastern and Western churches, the legitimacy of infant baptism, or the question of confession outside the confessional.

There would be no point in devoting what follows to listing the innumerable names from all the churches and increasingly from all parts of the world which have represented the theological *oikoumene* in our issues, nor to enumerate all the subjects tackled by these contributors—however enlightening such a conspectus might be with regard to the way our thinking has developed. But twenty years later we need to pay special consideration to our beginnings, shaped by the Vatican II revolution. We do not forget the dreams of our youth.

As early as 1968 a whole issue provided well-founded information on the question of apostolic succession, which as is well known represents the major reason for the lack of eucharistic communion between the different Christian churches. The ecumenical consensus apparent here about an apostolic succession of the entire Church and also about a special apostolic succession of Church leaders, prophets and teachers, and what was worked out about a possible apostolic succession outside the chain of layings-on of hands and about Protestant and Anglican orders, has meanwhile all been duly confirmed by numerous official joint ecumenical commissions established by the different churches. It should not be forgotten that already in this issue a positive attitude was taken towards the position of women in the Church's ministry long before *Concilium* devoted an issue edited by women to the question of women in the Church.

We theologians were at that time, of course, already aware of the unexpressed but effective anti-ecumenical strategy of delay conducted by the Roman Curia, a strategy with which numerous episcopates were quick voluntarily to ally themselves: this was more convenient and did not create any difficulties with the Church's headquarters, where (particularly in the Holy Office, now renamed the Congregation for the Doctrine of the Faith for opportunistic reasons) what prevailed was still not an ecumenically-minded Catholic theology but the Roman-oriented neo-scholasticism. In our journal we therefore supported right from the start efforts from below, from the grass-roots, against these reactionary tendencies from above. 'Courage needed'—for ecumenical experimentation—was the subject of the 1969 issue, with the aim of providing theological backing for the pressing desire for intercommunion, for joint biblical work and for ecumenical corrections in preaching, as well as encouraging ecumenical work at parish level, the ecumenical integration of theological faculties, and ecumenical co-operation by the churches on matters of public concern.

What became more and more clear at the end of the 1960s was that large sections of the hierarchy and of the theological community were drifting apart. This had the effect of encouraging internal emigration—or even leaving the Church—among the most actively conciliar-minded of the people of God. The situation was all the worse because meanwhile, in the wake of the student movement of 1968, there had been a fundamental social change both in Europe and in North America. As a result in the 1970 issue, entitled *Post-Ecumenical Christianity*, one could ask oneself with Yves Congar: 'Do the new problems of our secular world make ecumenism irrelevant?' Congar's negative answer to this question was confirmed by competent Orthodox, Protestant and Anglican theologians. With Walter Kasper and Johannes Remmers (who at this time was providing backing in the field of Orthodox theology in this section) I was able to establish a consensus with regard both to hopes and to complaints: (1) there has been a successful breakthrough into an open ecumenical future; (2) doctrinal differences have receded into the background; (3) the Church 'systems' are lagging far behind theology—the papacy is the chief difficulty for ecumenical agreement, as Paul VI himself had admitted.

But it was not for this reason that *Concilium* devoted its 1971 issue on ecumenism to *A Papal Primacy?*. The complex of problems had been formulated by a former member of *Concilium*'s board of editorial directors, Charles Davis, who shortly before had left the ministry of the Catholic Church precisely because of renewed set-backs to a development in the direction of reform. Both the report on the state of the question in exegesis and the various historical analyses in this issue make visible the extent of the distinction to be drawn between a pastoral Petrine ministry that can be defended on the basis of the New Testament and the papacy as it has developed, grown and indeed become deformed in history along juridical, centralising and triumphalist lines: what became clear once again was Rome's decisive share in the responsibility for the split with the Eastern Churches and with those of the Reformation. But this issue was not content just with criticism: the positive significance of a 'centre of communication', a ministry of pastoral leadership in the Church was brought out by several contributors. And the question was put to the non-Catholic churches whether a Petrine ministry in the Church could not indeed mean something. John XXIII had here shown a practical way forward into the future, whilst respecting many indisputable boundaries: how an ecumenical pope could be.

There were admittedly few traces at the start of the 1970s of this kind of charismatic Petrine ministry. The section on ecumenism, however, continued patiently and firmly on its theological path. Having already provided an issue on apostolic succession, we now had an issue edited by Walter Kasper that was explicitly devoted to the 'mutual recognition of ministries'. How, theologically and practically, could we arrive at a mutual recognition of ministries? There was indeed no lack of theological and practical proposals. And in the same issue a number of contributors were able to present an imposing array of documentation about the various dialogues that had meanwhile been taking place between different churches on the ministry and recognition of ministries: Catholic-Lutheran, Anglican-Catholic, Anglican-Methodist; inter-Church talks in France, the Netherlands and the United States. But how much longer must one ask oneself why in practice more does not occur between the different churches? Ecumenical theology—what for?

If it were increasingly a question of polarisation within the Catholic Church, in sharp contrast to the days of John XXIII and the Second Vatican Council, this had to be attributed primarily to the resistance, not to say obstruction of Rome. 'A risk of factions in the Church' was the question that occupied us quite explicitly in 1973. Already a schism was apparent on the right by the traditionalists led by Archbishop Lefebvre. To the honour of the theologians of the 'left', not least those of *Concilium* (who would regard themselves as being of the centre), it must be said that no split has taken place on this wing. On the basis of the New Testament and Church history this issue endorsed the legitimacy of opposition and contestation within the Church but rejected any schism, even only potential schism. Indeed, such important churchmen as Cardinal Suenens, the two successive general secretaries of the World Council of Churches, Visser 't Hooft and Philip Potter, and the president of the University of Notre Dame, Theodore Hesburgh, were asked to answer the question: 'How can we avoid unnecessary polarisation?'. My own synthesis at the conclusion of the issue reached three conclusions: (1) in certain situations the formation of factions or at least groupings is unavoidable; (2) nevertheless, factions and groupings should be avoided as much as possible in the Church; (3) pluralism between the churches should develop into pluralism within the Church.

Two years later, in 1975, with reference to the possibility of a new pontificate, a special issue was devoted to 'Church Renewal and the Petrine Ministry at the End of the Twentieth Century'. I myself had suggested that my name (my book, *Infallible? An Enquiry*, had appeared in 1970) should not appear as a lure on the cover. Giuseppe Alberigo and Walter Kasper were responsible for this issue, which in general continued the line taken to date on the renewal of the Church, with admittedly the greatest concentration on the pope's function as bishop of Rome. It was launched at a press conference in Rome: the contributors' ideas were taken up with interest by the press but completely ignored by the Curia. What still hung in the balance under the intellectual and often sceptically self-questioning pope of that time became completely evident under his second successor.

Concilium did not need a Luther centenary to provide an ecumenical appraisal of the Reformer's significance. Indeed, the questions raised in the 1976 issue, *Luther—Then and Now*, are more topical than ever today: why was Luther not able to succeed? Why was Luther not understood at the time? What was the connection between the doctrine of justification and criticism of the Church, theology and politics, faith and Church, Gospel and papacy? How is Luther judged today, and how is he judged outside Lutheranism? There were contributions from theologians from various churches, with the last word being left to Catholic theologians, especially the prominent Luther scholar

O. H. Pesch. Two things became clear from this issue. First, Catholic research on Luther has made decisive progress over the last decades in both history and theology. Secondly, though the official Catholic Church has revised its verdict on the person of Luther (the pope had postive things to say about the Reformer when he visited Mainz in 1980), it has hardly begun to draw the practical consequences from its theology.

It can hardly be overlooked that in the meantime we had dealt with the vast bulk of the classical list of controversial theological questions between the Christian churches, particularly since a subsequent issue in 1979, *The Holy Spirit in Conflict,* was devoted to discussion of yet another central subject of controversy between Christians (the Son and the Spirit—Orthodoxy; the Word and the Spirit—Protestantism; ministry and the Spirit—Catholicism; and the Spirit and the spirits—the charismatic movement).

3. FUNDAMENTAL ECUMENICAL QUESTIONS

The section on ecumenism, therefore, decided to pay more attention to the fundamental ecumenical questions that the churches had in common rather than to the differences between them. 'What are we on earth for?': at the public question and answer session on the state of Christendom in Munich in 1975 a journalist asked the members of the *Concilium* editorial board, 'Does the old question from the catechism still apply? How would you answer it today?' And in the event Luther's question about God's grace had meanwhile to a considerable extent been taken over by the question about the meaning of life. The answers from the different denominations in this 1977 issue make it clear how fruitful it is when the different Christian traditions question and enrich each other and also when non-theologians have their say—including the Polish poet Jan Dobraczyński, the North American writer John Garvey, the Nicaraguan poet, who has since become world famous, Ernesto Cardenal, the African John Mbiti and the Chinese Julia Ching.

A similar consideration of fundamental questions was attempted in 1978 with the issue entitled *An Ecumenical Creed?* The question is indeed worth thinking about and was put in the form of a questionnaire: What should form part of a future ecumenical creed? Both convergence and divergence appeared in the answers from the different churches. In his synthesis Lukas Vischer, for many years the worthy secretary of the World Council of Churches' Faith and Order commission, called for two things: the development of the consensus that already existed, and joint anticipatory profession of faith on as many occasions as possible—the more freely the churches that are still divided decided to profess their faith jointly, the quicker will communion grow among them.

It is in this context that one should see the 1980 issue, *Conflicting Ways of Interpreting the Bible*. In this not only is the necessity of the historical-critical method advocated but at the same time new forms of linguistic, materialistic and psycho-analytical interpretation are presented. At the same time we were interested in how such different constituencies as Jewish exegesis, black theology and feminism accepted Scripture today and how grass-roots communities in Latin America dealt with the Bible. Dialogue with the Bible, dialogue about the Bible and dialogue with him to whose truth the Bible bears witness remain the heart of Christian ecumenism. This issue was also the only occasion when I have spoken out in my own case in an issue of *Concilium* devoted to ecumenism, with 'A Letter on Christology and Infallibility' prompted by the intervention in December 1979 of the Roman Doctrinal Congregation.

Meanwhile it had become clear, not least through the active intervention of the Roman doctrinal authorities against various theologians, especially those attached to *Concilium*, that the period of conciliar renewal was finally closed but that the long inter-regnum of post-conciliar stagnation was also over and that with the new pontificate, despite all the commitment to social justice outside the Church, a period of Roman Catholic restoration had been initiated within the Church. This did not stop *Concilium* from going on working in loyalty to its name and its programme and tackling the new problems head on in the issues devoted to ecumenism, even if with a certain delay due to planning two years in advance. Since these latest issues will be fresh in our readers' memories, it is enough to cite the subjects they dealt with: *Who Has the Say in the Church?* (1981), *The Right to Dissent* (1982) and *Mary in the Churches* (1983).

4. WERE WE ON THE RIGHT PATH?

Who would dare give a positive answer to this kind of question without any ifs and buts? The various individual contributions and issues have been too varied and indeed in many things too open to question. But as far as concerns the general line followed by *Concilium* and its section on ecumenism, one ought to say: John XXIII and Vatican II were on the right path when they took the way of conciliar renewal and ecumenical understanding instead of that of counter-Reformation restoration (and indeed none too early but four hundred years too late in so many questions such as the language of the liturgy, communion under both kinds, and dialogue). *Concilium* and its section on ecumenism have consistently continued on this path in the spirit of the Council. For us the Council is not an end but a beginning. And to the extent that this international theological journal is inspired by the spirit of the Council it is on the right path.

Have we been successful? Success is no criterion of truth. But is it a criterion for effectiveness? I do not doubt that the influence of *Concilium* has been considerable on Catholic and on many non-Catholic theologians, and also indirectly on the grass-roots of the Church. The *Concilium* team represents the only internationally organised group of Catholic theologians which has at its disposal an organ published throughout the world in many different languages and which was able to collect the signatures of 1,360 Catholic professors of theology for a statement as important as that issued in 1968 on freedom in theology—something that did not lack impact in Rome. But looking at it as a whole can one identify an influence by *Concilium* on the Church's leadership in Rome and in the various different countries round the world? While exceptions prove the rule, this one must take leave to doubt.

But does this apply only to *Concilium*? Does this not apply to theology generally as it is made use of in practice in the Catholic Church (leaving on one side, of course, the various tame court theologians attached to the Roman and episcopal curias)? Cannot it be compared to the research department of a large, highly bureaucratic and centralised corporation, regarded as fundamentally disruptive by the production department and especially by the conservative-minded central management? This research department spends its time, in the management's view, unearthing 'new notions' and 'troublesome bright ideas' that demand not just the change of many methods and new investment but also the change of personal attitudes: getting rid of one's fear of what is new, fighting one's own spiritual inertia and plain indolence, often, too, coming to terms with one's own ignorance and giving up power to subordinate offices. . . . Why not, they ask themselves in the executive suite, stick to the tried and trusted methods of the past and the customs one has come to value, at least as long as the whole thing goes on ticking over?

There are hardly any industrial corporations that have a highly qualified research department but ignore its findings: events catch up with them and they quickly find themselves in the red. Competition does not let up. The Catholic Church, at least in the denominationally divided highly industrialised countries of the West, has long since been in the red. The capital of trust that accrued to it in the time of John XXIII and the Council has mostly been squandered. People try to hide this by means of public relations and enormous Church rallies for congresses and papal visits: in many people's view, a short-lived burst of enthusiasm without any visible lasting effect. At all events everyday life at parish level has quite a different appearance: fewer and fewer people going to church, fewer and fewer priests, fewer and fewer baptisms, fewer and fewer marriages in church, fewer and fewer young people taking any interest. . . .

Does this mean we theologians should just be resigned to all this? No, many of us as long ago as 1972 signed the 'Appeal against resignation' that also emanated from *Concilium*. We have tried, untiringly and patiently, like so many of our unappreciated predecessors (from Origen and Thomas Aquinas to Teilhard de Chardin, Yves Congar and Henri de Lubac), to provide, in difficult times, the theological foundations for a new and better future.

5. TO FURTHER SHORES

In the section on ecumenism we shall continue in the future to provide theological coverage of the development of ecumenical relations between the different churches. But this ecumenism *ad intra* requires increasingly urgently to be complemented by a ecumenism *ad extra*: the *oikoumene* of the world religions.

Here the section will be making for new shores. Already a foretaste was provided in 1974 by the issue devoted to ecumenical relations between Christians and Jews, while the section on fundamental theology devoted its 1976 issue to Christians and Moslems. Previously, as far as the Jews were concerned, there had been a lot of talk about the centuries of Christian anti-Semitism and the Nazi holocaust, but the central theological differences had hardly been tackled. In our issue they were brought into the centre of the dialogue and both Jewish and Christian theologians were asked for contributions on questions like the meaning of the law in Judaism and Christianity, the structure and content of Jewish and Christian worship, sin and forgiveness in Judaism and Christianity. The Jew Samuel Sandmel answered the question, 'Which Jew is a good Jew?' and the Christian Jan Milic Lochmann the question, 'Which Christian is a good Christian?'.

But of course this can only be a beginning. However, this kind of concentration on the central theological differences between the major religions—with Hinduism, Buddhism and the Chinese religions now considered alongside Judaism and Islam—will be our guiding line in the future too. In this world-wide religious perspective it will be necessary to consider anew the entire Christian dogmatic heritage in the light of the world religions. If *Concilium* continues for another twenty years, one can hope for some small degree of progress in this field too.

Twenty years of ecumenical theology—what for? Ultimately, in my view, what ecumenical theology is concerned with is to make our churches and our theologies more credible: in our eyes, in the eyes of the men and women with whom we live throughout the world, but above all when measured against the Gospel of Jesus Christ as our ultimate norm. Only when ecumenical theology regards it as its most specific task to serve the men and women in all the different churches and increasingly, too, in all the different religions will it have not only a past but also a future.

Translated by Robert Nowell

Casiano Floristán

Spirituality. A Retrospective and Prospective View

THE NINETEEN issues of *Concilium* devoted to Spirituality show a wide spectrum of theoretical and practical reflection on Christian life. For an overall view of these reflections, I propose to divide this synthesis into three parts: the applicability of Christian spirituality, its overall nature and its characteristics.

1. THE APPLICABILITY OF SPIRITUALITY

'At the Second Vatican Council the Church has taken cognizance of a new form of existence in the world', Christian Duquoc stated in the *Preface* to the first issue devoted to Spirituality.[1] If Vatican II has been both the starting-point and the shutdown for all sorts of theological and pastoral reflections, its implications in the field of spirituality have been as obvious as any.

Until the 1950s, spirituality, with its numerous schools and tendencies, was an undisputed Christian preserve; the only debate was about methods and stresses within the different ecclesiastical and monastic enclaves concerned with the religious life.[2] Essays in secular spirituality, based on the very condition of lay people placed squarely within the world, were before the Council sporadic incursions into a professional field which had the effect of broadening the concept of Christian life.[3]

The 1960s produced a profound change in the understanding of spirituality, questioning it on the subject not only of its methods and modes, but of its very meaning. These were the years of the Council (1962-5) and of Medellín (1968), of the challenge to the system, of the Prague spring and the student uprising in France in May 1968, of Latin American liberation movements and the reinterpretation of secularisation, of Christian-Marxist dialogues and the emergence of the base communities with their valuation of popular Catholicism based on the people as active subject. The spirituality of the immediate post-conciliar period emancipated itself from the 'mental and institutional complex of Christendom' (Chenu), laid stress on a new 'way of experiencing the world as the privileged setting for sanctification' (Geffré) and saw itself as 'no longer detached from the heart of faith, but as the most integral, personal expression of the total mystery of Christ in (their) existence' (Duquoc). Criticisms of Christian spirituality based on psycho-analysis, Marxist analysis and the commitment to liberation forced it to shed all its former tinges of alienation.[4]

The 1970s produced a religious or spiritual awakening characterised by movements that 'within the Church or alongside it, witness to the need for an almost mystical fervour to make the message of the Gospel understood'.[5] As V. Codina expressed it: 'There was a discovery of the gratuitous and the festive, the ritual and symbolic dimension of human life came to the fore again, "homo faber" was succeeded by "homo ludens", the "secular city" by "jester festivals", Utopian revolutionaries by neo-mystics of all kinds. There was a new taste for spiritual or religious experience, Oriental mysticism, ecstasy, hallucinatory "trips", a return to nature and a desire for ecological communion. Within Christianity we see the upsurge of charismatic renewal movements and prayer groups. Because the belief in unlimited progress had reached a crisis and because of the disenchantment when it proved impossible to transform structures, it seemed that there was no alternative but flight into religious experience and cosy private intimacy, a falling back into the warmth of prayer. Of course this religious revival was ambivalent and required spiritual discernment'.[6]

Now we are well into the 1980s. There is no simple diagnosis of Christian spirituality as it exsits in today's society, any more than there is a simple one of society today as a whole. In opposition to the present concentration of potentially destructive forces (the arms race, the control of vital geo-political and economic fields, the increasing centralisation of capitalism, etc.), ecological and pacifist movements spring up on a world-wide scale, pointing out unequivocally the ecological degradation of the planet as a place of human habitation, with the resulting mass starvation of the Third World, and the danger of military adventures escalating into full-scale nuclear war. The great powers are turned in on themselves, preoccupied with defending their own interests or the privileges of small groups; they and other governments incapable of rising above national preoccupations forget the needs of humanity as a whole. This dangerous restriction of view brings the corollary of alienation of people's minds, so that they lose interest in seeking political solutions, as well as in organised religion.

The Catholic Church, excessively concentrated on its papal head, seems concerned only with re-establishing Catholic unity on the basis of a resurgence of discipline (the new *Codex*), morality (traditional ethics whole and entire) and dogma (a return to orthodoxy), expounded in frequent discourses alike in their forgettableness and only occasionally bearing directly on the spiritual awareness of humankind.

There are signs of spiritual renewal in small scattered groups, communities and movements, a *remnant* for future generations, but who can tell whether they are simply the *residue*, in some cases, of a glorious past, or, in others, the *seeds* of a promising future? Perhaps the era of ideologies is coming to an end, to be replaced by one of mystagogies. The present younger generation is apparently more contemplative than active, more mystical than political, stressing the transcendental at the expense of social concerns, the opposite to what happened two decades ago.[7]

2. THE OVERALL NATURE OF SPIRITUALITY

The term 'spirituality', derived from the concept of 'spirit', has a number of connotations attaching to its original meaning. Opposed to the corporal, spirit is understood as something ethereal, untouchable and invisible. As a proper noun it designates the third person of the Blessed Trinity, scarcely recognised and worshipped by the faithful. By extension it is something linked to the ecstatic experience of an individual (mystic) or a group (charismatic). If Christianity is taken as a religion of the spirit, spirituality has been justly criticised as a totally negative attitude to material, bodily and instinctive reality.

What needs saying at once is that the concept of spirituality is both recent and imprecise. Duquoc says that it 'refers to Christian life in so far as we wish to discover in this life certain directives by which to guide ourselves in practice'.[8] Hans Urs von Balthasar defines it as 'that basic practical or existential attitude of man which is the consequence and expression of the way in which he understands his religious—or more generally, his ethically committed—existence; the way in which he acts and reacts habitually throughout his life according to his objective and ultimate insights and decisions'.[9] A. M. Besnard calls it 'on the one hand . . . the structuring of an adult personality in faith according to one's proper genius, vocation and charismatic gifts; and on the other hand according to the laws of the universal Christian mystery'.[10]

According to François Vandenbroucke, 'spirituality is first of all the science of the reaction of the religious conscience vis-a-vis the object of faith—this is the intellectual aspect; secondly it is the science of those human acts that have a special reference to God, that is, asceticism and mysticism'.[11]

If we look at the specific characteristics of post-conciliar spiritual movements, we can pick out those notes that define Christian spirituality today.[12]

(a) Spirituality, understood as the organised methodology of religious wisdom and the loving, burning quest for the Absolute, goes beyond the confines of Christianity. There are Christian and non-Christian spiritualities.[13]

(b) Christian spirituality has a *christocentric* origin. In other words, the Christian gives ultimate meaning, through identifying with the historical passion of Jesus and with his resurrection, to that dynamism charged with meaning and which cannot be evaded without losing his human condition and denying the Christian meaning of this world.[14]

(c) The *Gospel* is the norm and test of all Christian spirituality, which is based on Jesus' loving approach to the Father and the Holy Spirit. Christian spirituality is first and foremost evangelical.[15]

(d) Christian spirituality integrates the historical background which conditions a person's thought, feelings and behaviour into his spiritual progress. In other words: the fact that the Christian lives in the *world* is constituent of his spirituality, since his manner of living in society is his prime route to holiness, since Christianity is not contempt for the world, but its assumption, consecration and perfecting.[16]

(e) The experience of belonging to a believing *community*, originally a liturgical community though not confined to liturgical expression, is a part of Christian spirituality. This link with a community embraces all sectors of human life, within the context of faith, providing common objectives, interests and goals which enable believers to see their world and their own history in the light of the mystery of the risen Christ. Christian spirituality repudiates *individualism*; it tends to unfold in cells of life in brotherly community.[17]

(f) In opposition to the private nature of spirituality during the nineteenth and early twentieth centuries, we must stress the totalising nature of Christian faith, which makes no distinction between interiority and exteriority. Christian spirituality overcomes the opposition between *private* and *public* spheres. In this way, there is stress on the natural home of spirituality being in the most socially and politically committed Christian lives, and recognition of the social and political implications of particular spiritual currents.[18]

(g) Spirituality is related to theology,[19] despite the fact that the debate between masters of spirituality and of theology has been a difficult one throughout the history of the Church. Let us get rid of one illusion: some people imagine innocently that theology is a royal road to an integrated life in the meeting with Christ. So they demand immediate pastoral usefulness, applicable spiritual direction and commitment to changing the world from the theologian. Others, with a pre-conciliar mentality,

E

understand theology as a material echo or systematised repetition of the episcopal or papal *magisterium*. They forget that the task of the theologian consists in linking the world and the word of God, with a link which can be broken or stretched by 'this continually renewed tension between a divine Word that pulls man up short, that takes hold of him and saves him, and a human world which puts God on trial'.[20] The theologian's job is not to justify present practice nor to offer immediate certainties, but to collate—critically—the Word of God and the 'signs of the times', which are often out of step with one another, since human questioning is often atheistic and faith is not full clarity.

Spirituality, through exercises and experiences, using a theological background, seeks to shed light on and mature the applicability of Christian religious decisions to persons and groups. It does not move on a *noetic* level (as a pure quest for truth), nor in the *ethical* field (as a matter of taking decisions from commitment), but in a predominantly *aesthetic* and gratuitous dimension in which personal emotions, affectivity and sensibility come into play. Spirituality, as a believing exercise, is nevertheless situated at the centre of human existence, where love springs from and where love is stronger than death. A person's spiritual dimension reaches into the depths of human existence (J.-M. Castillo).

3. CHARACTERISTICS OF SPIRITUALITY

By means of experiences and exercises, spirituality tries to form in the believing person or group a series of *Christian reflexes* in relation to the basic virtues which go to make up holiness.

(*a*) We are still a long way from being able to understand certain models of holiness, without on the other hand knowing how to define the characteristics of the 'saint of today'. The issue of *Concilium* devoted to this subject (1979) shows that the definition of holiness has gone through considerable changes in the course of history: 'To gain official entry on the basis of the record of achievements in the church on earth . . . is a matter of having matched up with a certain notion of holiness prevalent among the Catholic people or the courts in Rome',[21] without forgetting that the Church readily promotes its servants to the kingdom of God.

It has not always been the sanctity of Jesus that has formed the type of Christian saint. As J. Rovira Belloso said of Jesus' holiness: (*a*) '(It) was applied to the real life of his day, not kept aside from its history'; (*b*) '(It) accepts the evil in history and, prophetically and actually, challenges the agents of evil in the world'; (*c*) 'Jesus takes the particular situation of individuals, relates to them and in them creates the image of the new man, called to fullness, which consists in likeness to the image of the new man who Christ is'.[22] In stark contrast to these statements is a model of holiness for religious or priestly life (the laity not being called to perfection) prevalent since the seventeenth century, which is characterised by affirmation of the primacy of religious and sacral values: extolling the need for a contemplative life; the values of sacrifice and generosity; asceticism to form strong characters and virtually no grounding in the New Testament.[23] The *ultima ratio* underlying this conception of holiness, and therefore of spirituality, is based on separation or segregation, on the sacred-profane antithesis, on emphasis on the spirit to the detriment of the carnal, on the celestial as opposed to the terrestial.

(*b*) The soul of Christian spirituality resides in *prayer*. *Concilium* has devoted two issues (in 1972 and 1982, with ten years between them) to this theme. While prayer was a traditional Christian exercise (remember the Lenten triad of prayer, fasting and alms-giving), and one that went unquestioned in the past, it is now an uncommon practice, with no social acceptability. There are those who say people pray more now than they did ten years ago. It may be that for various cultural and evangelical reasons, the quality of prayer has improved, if not its quantity. *Concilium* has moved from the problem of prayer (what use is it?) to the need, which is not questioned, for learning how to pray. From these issues, the following four statements stand out:

(i) *Prayer is an exercise of faith and an act inseparable from conversion.* 'The believer calls on God in order that Jesus' freedom as Son may become his freedom; the believer begs God to give him the Spirit of Jesus so that he may be converted. Prayer is the act by which one abandons oneself in order to let oneself be seized by the freedom of the Spirit. The cry forced from us by our suffering because the kingdom has not come, or by our alienation because freedom is a promise, expresses our situation before God; we do not require of him either an increase of power or a privileged status, but the freedom which comes from the Spirit. Paradoxically, we ask him for the power to be ourselves by allowing him to be God for us. In this way we become sons, that is capable of not being in any way rivals of the Father, responsible for ourselves, open to love.'[24]

(ii) *The action of the Spirit is the basis of Christian prayer.* 'The most important part in Christian prayer is played not by the one praying, but by the Spirit, who prays in him, baptises his attitude as a human being, and, by passing through his life, makes it an offering or "cult" '.[25]

(iii) *The liturgical prayer of the Church is the referral model of all Christian prayer.* 'Tradition developed the eucharistic and penitential prayer through the divine office and the *lectio divina* with readings, hymns, psalms and canticles. This way of praying, which goes on in monasteries, is beginning to be introduced gradually into Christian groups as a basic procedure for community and personal prayer. Holy Scripture as the essential nourishment for prayer has a predominant place.'[26]

(iv) *No genuine Christian prayer is possible without spiritual experience of the Lord of the poor.* 'In the cry of the poor we hear the traditional prayer which recurs in the psalms, the prayers of Jesus, the texts of the primitive Church and the experiences of popular piety. We learn to pray with the poor and from the point of view of the poor. In other words it is a question of being *contemplative in the work of liberation.* Hence we discover a new symbiosis of the old formula: *ora et labora*, ie., pray *by* action, *in* action and *with* action.'[27]

(c) In Christian life today, because of the tensions produced by praxis, two basic poles have emerged which set their seal on two spiritual tendencies which are frequently opposed to one another and rarely seem to converge: the *spirituality of commitment* (based on ethical considerations of liberation of the whole person) and the spirituality of the *feast* (based on a playful attitude of anticipated transcendence).[28]

Describing the marks of a universally human spirituality, Hans Urs von Balthasar pointed to three forms of spirituality: (i) the *transcendental* (going out of oneself towards the absolute) the starting-point of which is Plato's spiritualisation of *eros*, Augustine's of *desiderium*, and Thomas Acquinas' of *amor-appetitus*; (ii) the *activist*, or spirituality of objective commitment, finding its field of action, accreditation, source of knowledge and purification in the world (Aristotle); (iii) the spirituality of *passivity*, characterised by the indifference of the absolute *logos* to all objections raised by finite reason (Stoic *apatheia*).[29]

Plato of course distinguished between *teoria* (the contemplation of ideas that are eternal, subsistent, behind reality), which was a proper occupation for free men, and *poiesis* (practice relative to shifting, fragile and relative realities), the proper concern of slaves. Aristotle's introduction of *praxis* as a political and moral activity enriched the concept of work designed to transform the social environment, but theory still remained primary. So in the middle ages the *contemplative life* (which related to liberal studies) was superior to the *active life* (connected with servile works). Later development of this antithesis after the Reformation—without forgetting that the Benedictines had always held to both: *ora et labora*—pushed Christian spirituality in the direction of exalting the previously despised areas of work and world (family as opposed to celibacy, manual work as opposed to intellectual activity and social responsibility as opposed to sacramental ritualism) till the new synthesis put forward by Ignatius was reached: action, which is itself a setting for union with God and sanctification, is not opposed to contemplation. Hence the axiom '*in actione contemplativus*' which today in Latin America is translated into 'contemplatives in political action', in action that transforms history (Gutiérrez). *A time of prayer*, as practised in the base communities, goes alongside the *time of solidarity* with the poor in their struggle to live—which can lead to the *time of martyrdom* as the supreme act of witness to faith. 'Nowhere in Latin America,' Gutiérrez states, 'do people pray with more fervour and joy in the midst of suffering than in these communities set among the poor. This is an act of gratitude to and hope in the Spirit who sets us free and leads us to the full truth.'[30]

(*d*) The *discernment* or *discretion* of spirits, described by St Ignatius in the *Spiritual Exercises* in a typical and special way, is a traditional Christian task, belonging to the deepest and most ancient basis of spirituality.[31] The 'Ritual of Pentinence' (no. 10) states that discernment is 'final knowledge of God's action in the hearts of men, a gift of the Holy Spirit and a fruit of charity'. Therefore, 'It is not surprising that discernment should be related to personal conversion and communal reconciliation. Discernment and discretion are something other than just understanding, interpreting; they have to do with the transformation of men.'[32]

The following conclusions emerge from a reading of the issue devoted to discernment:

(i) Christian discernment is 'the particular quest for the will of God, not only to understand it but also to carry it out. Discernment is, therefore, to be understood not only literally but as a process in which the will of God carried out also verifies the will of God thought'.[33] To sum up, discernment is 'a fundamental choice, a prophetic task, a practical decision, virtue and charism. It demands a human interpretative model and an evangelical programme of action leading to the actual realisation of the kingdom of God.'[34]

(ii) Christian discernment should not be restricted to the spiritual life or the inner life of pious souls, but is an ecclesial and community concern. Its final objective is to help bring the kingdom of God into actual being. This is a complex and global process which depends on present-day situations, historical inheritances and psychological conditionings. Discerning, according to Jesus' criterion, requires great docility to the Holy Spirit and a clear option for the poor and oppressed. Finally, the subject who discerns is the people of God in a state of community or Church.

(*e*) Christian *obedience*, today, like all the virtues, situated in a context of socio-cultural secularisation and within a pluralist Church, split into different theological, moral and spiritual tendencies, seeks its roots in Christ 'obedient unto death'. Christian obedience can be rediscovered in its clarity and entirety only by starting from a correct christology. Naturally, Christ's obedience to the demands of the kingdom and the Father is a paradigm and an example, but it cannot be imitated. Nevertheless, despite the mediations inherent in faith, which provides the setting for Christian obedience, we need to bring out the various applications of this obedience, so as not to reduce it to mere acceptance of a totalitarian power. The main ones are these:

(i) The act of obeying is a human act enacted by a person as creative subject, with his own autonomy, conscience, freedom and responsibility. To obey 'inhumanly' is not Christian.

(ii) The believer obeys as a *member of the Church* within a Christian community. He is not a mere subject of the hierarchy, but a brother in the common faith, in a relationship of obedience to those who hold responsible office in the Church and whose task it is to carry out the functions of the Spirit. Recourse must be had to those brothers in the community or the congregation who are most open to the demands of the Spirit. Taking obedience out of its context of ecclesial communion detracts from its Christian connotation.

(iii) Once Christian obedience is seen to be in the *line of faith*, all believers—from last to first—are obedient to God, who has revealed himself through Jesus the Christ on his evangelical road to the fulfilment of the kingdom and complete communion with the Father. Christian obedience is a common task, to be carried out by all believers, since all—though with different charisms and ministries—possess the Holy Spirit. Reducing one part of the Church to silence on the pretext of absolute obedience distorts the Christian act of obeying.

(iv) There is often an *ecclesial tension* produced between established norms and the promptings of the Spirit. Sometimes obedience is impossible through over-commanding or bad commanding. It can also fail because no one is exercising authority. Any conflict between Christians requires recourse to competent colleagues and experts, within the context of a genuinely evangelical and human 'fraternal correction'.

(v) Christian obedience is not merely a passive virtue proper to subjects subordinate to those who hold the office of command. Christian obedience does not seek personal sanctifications but the fruitfulness of Christian life in society. Christian obedience is an *active virtue* because it is faithfulness to all the requirements of the Spirit of Jesus.[35]

(*f*) Post-conciliar attempts to define a new spirituality are still fragmentary and insufficiently united. The last few years, corresponding to the end of the pontificate of Paul VI and the beginning of that of John Paul II, have seen Christian spirituality oscillate between *turning inward* (a return to the spiritual restoration of the Baroque age, such as characterised the nineteenth century and the first half of the twentieth) and *renewal* (acceptance of an incarnate, committed, evangelical and missionary Christianity). The following are symptoms of a new spirituality which have been suggested in the pages of *Concilium*:

(i) The preferential option for the poor and for those who are fighting for the future of man and for his overall liberation, with a consequent distancing of the Church from the ruling and 'conservative' classes.[36]

(ii) The ecumenical discovery of Eastern spiritualities, particularly those of Asia (Hinduism, Buddhism, Taoism), brought about by cultural and religious interchange between East and West.[37]

(iii) The rise of new spiritual *movements*, such as the charismatic revival,[38] or the renewal of traditional ones,[39] has shown young people—whose culture is difficult and volatile—new ways to spiritual awareness.[40]

(iv) To sum up, post-conciliar spirituality is evolving in a climate of debate between mystical tradition and historical actuality, efficacy and gratuitousness, suffering and joy, spiritual infancy and critical maturity.[41] The new charisms have 'emphasised the necessity of mysticism in a Church devoted to the word or to action.[42]

Translated by Paul Burns

Notes

Translator's note: References throughout are to the *Spirituality* issues of *Concilium*. Since in the early years the method of numbering and the page numbers varied between the English and American editions, the year of publication has been judged sufficient common reference. Page references from 1965-9 are to the English edition.

1. C. Duquoc, *Preface* 1965, at p. 3. Duquoc has been Executive Editor of the Spirituality section from the founding of the Review till the present, with first Claude Geffré as Assistant (eight issues), then Casiano Floristán (ten issues).

2. See B. Jiménez Duque and E. O'Brien in 1966.

3. See C. Duquoc 'The Believer and Christian Existence' 1965, pp. 66-72; R. Bultot 'Terrestrial Reality and Lay Spirituality' 1966, pp. 23-30; Sr. A. Cunningham 'Complexity and Challenge: the American Catholic Layman' 1965, pp. 58-65; P. Mikat 'Collaboration between Clergy and Laity' 1965, pp. 34-38.

4. See E. Dussel and W. Ureña in 119 (1978), pp. 47 and 61.

5. C. Duquoc, Editorial 89 (1973).

6. V. Codina 'Learning to Pray Together with the Poor. A Christian Necessity' 159 (1982), p. 3.

7. J. M. González Ruiz 'A Spirituality for a Time of Uncertainty' 1966; C. Geffré 'The Tension between Desacralisation and Spirituality' 1966; M. de Certeau 'Culture and Spiritual Experience' 1966; R. Rémond 'The Spiritual Crisis at the Heart of the "Consumer Society"' 1969; F. de Hoogh 'Prayer in a Secularised World' 1969; C. Geffré 'Secularisation and the Future of the Religious Life' 1969; F. Kerr 'The Latent Spirituality of the Counter-Culture' 69 (1971).

8. C. Duquoc, Editorial (1965).

9. H. Urs von Balthasar 'The Gospel as Norm and Test of all Spirituality in the Church' 1965, p. 5.

10. A. Besnard 'Tendencies of Contemporary Spirituality' 1965, p. 14.

11. F. Vandenbroucke 'Spirituality and Spiritualities' 1965, p. 28.

12. See Besnard, in the articles cited in note 10.

13. See E. Cornélis 'Christian Spirituality and non-Christian Spiritualities' 1965.

14. C. Duquoc 'The Believer and Christian Existence' 1965; see H. Urs von Bathasar 'Closeness to God' 1967.

15. See von Balthasar 'The Gospel as Norm . . .', the article cited in note 9; G. Bouwman 'Is the Bible still a Valid Spiritual Guide?' 1969.

16. See C. Geffré 'The Tension . . .', the article cited in note 7, 1966.

17. See B. Cooke 'Existential Pertinence of Religion' 1966.

18. See 1971, edited by C. Geffré, esp. C. Duquoc 'Spirituality: a Private or Public Phenomenon?'.

19. See C. Duquoc 'Theology and Spirituality' 1966.

20. *Ibid*.

21. C. Duquoc, Editorial 129 (1979), at p. vii.

22. J. Rovira Belloso 'The Nature of Holiness in Jesus of Nazareth' 129 (1979), p. 3, at pp. 8-9.

23. F. Urbina 'Models of Priestly Holiness. A Bibliographical Review' 129 (1979), p. 88.

24. C. Duquoc, Editorial 79 (1972), at p. 10.

25. P. Jacquemont 'The Holy Spirit—Master of Prayer' 159 (1982), p. 23.

26. C. Floristán, Editorial 159 (1982); see J. Leclercq 'The Divine Office and *Lectio divina*' 159 (1982), p. 31.

27. C. Floristán, Editorial 159 (1982); see P. Jacquemont 'Is Action a Prayer?' 79 (1972), p. 39; V. Codina 'Learning to Pray together with the Poor' 159 (1982), p. 3.

28. Compare 1968, devoted basically to the 'feast' and 1975 (in the non-English language editions) on Conflicts.

29. H. Urs von Balthasar 'The Gospel as Norm. . . .' 1965, the article cited in note 9, pp. 7-8.

30. G. Gutiérrez 'Drink from your own Well' 159 (1982), p. 38; see G. Bessière 'Do Revolutionaries pray? Testimonies from South America' 79 (1972), p. 109; G. Remmert 'Spiritual Movements and Political Praxis' 89 (1973), p. 85; S. Galilea 'Spiritual Awakening and Movements of Liberation in Latin America' 89 (1973), p. 129; G. Gutiérrez 'Faith and Political Commitment' in the non-English language editions of 1975.

31. See 119 (1978) devoted to the discernment of spirits.

32. C. Floristán, Editorial 119 (1978).

33. J. Sobrino 'Following Jesus as Discernment' 119 (1978), p. 14.

34. C. Floristán, Editorial 119 (1978).

35. C. Floristán, Editorial 139 (1980).

36. See 1975 (in the non-English language editions) on the Life of Faith and Human Conflicts.

37. See J. A. Cuttat 'Christian Experience and Eastern Spirituality' (1969); A. Besnard 'The Influence of Asiatic Methods of Meditation' 79 (1972), p. 91; C. Murray Rogers 'Hindu Ashram Heritage: God's Gift to the Church' 1965; G. Siegmund and H. Dumoulin 'The Encounter with Buddhism' 1967; W. Johnston 'Dialogue with Zen' 1969; G. Neyrand 'Christianity in Japan' 1965; H. Waldenfels 'Christianity in the Spiritual Climate of Japan' 1966; P.-R. Cren 'Krishna's Flute' 79 (1972), p. 117.

38. See J. Massingberg Ford 'Pentecostal Catholicism' 79 (1972) p. 85; D. Gelpi 'American Pentecostalism' 89 (1973), p. 101; G. Combert & L. Fabre 'The Pentecostal Movement and the Gift of Healing' 99 (1974), p. 106.

39. R. Aubert 'Attempting to renew Monastic Life: the Brothers of the Virgin of the Poor' 1966; see also 89 (1973) on Movements of Religious Awakening.

40. See Doc. 'Christian Groups and their Ways of Life' 1968; L. & P. Mettler 'Forms of Religious Behaviour among the Younger Generation' 1969, and articles by W. Salters Stirling and D. Salman in the same issue.

41. See the special issues devoted to Suffering (in the non-English language editions) 1976, Discernment 119 (1978) and Obedience 139 (1980).

42. C. Duquoc, Editorial 109 (1977) and the whole issue, devoted to Charisms in the Church 109 (1977).

Jacques Pohier

Plurality and Communion? Conviction and Responsibility? Twenty Years of Moral Theology in *Concilium*

AT VATICAN II, no particular importance was accorded to Moral Theology. The Bishops rapidly dismissed the preparatory schemata *De ordine morali* as outdated in form and content, and concentrated on questions of dogma—particularly ones relating to ecclesiology—or questions of exegesis or liturgy. There were thus very few moral theologians among their experts, and when some were finally selected they were immediately set to work on *Gaudium et Spes*, the one important Vatican II text dealing specifically with Moral Theology. Mgr Philippe Delhaye, an expert on this and the ensuing period, claims that 'The consequences of the foregoing were, paradoxically, fortunate. The former casuistic moral theology disappeared almost completely. A new expression of the moral imperatives of the faith was to be found which enjoyed continuity with Scripture, dogma and the life of the Church: in short, by re-establishing contacts which the advocates of a renewed moral theology had hardly dared to suppose could be restored.'[1]

This, in fact, was the very tone of the first issues of moral theology in *Concilium*. We must note, however, that in the editorial of the first issue, Franz Böckle, first editor of the section, puts complementary stress on the other sources of theological anthropology (philosophy and human sciences), ecumenical dialogue with regard to ethics and the attention given to the way in which ethical questions were approached by the non-Christian world (all these being well in line with Vatican II). The first two issues (Vol. 5, No. 1, 1965, and Vol. 5, No. 2, 1966) differ from those subsequent in that they are not centred on one theme; in this way they effectively treat important, and sometimes hotly debated, subjects: in fundamental morality, questions on the natural law, the historicity of moral norms and the ethics of autonomy; in the life of the Church and of religious communities, questions on religious freedom, tolerance, authority and obedience; in specific morality, the concepts (already!) of war, peace and pacifism, the Third World and revolution, birth control, population explosion, marital problems, etc. I myself made no contribution to the section on morality; speaking twenty years later I can only marvel at the obvious perspicacity present in this choice of themes. The same goes for the central themes around which all the issues, from 1967 onwards, were entirely organised: ethical norms (Vol 5, No. 3, 1967); the contribution of the Church towards the ethics of society (Vol. 5, No. 4, 1968)—this theme was typical of the preoccupations of the period immediately after the Council; the role of manual and professional work in society (Vol. 5, No. 5, 1969); the institution of marriage (55, 1970); and the manipulation of the individual (65, 1977).

The Congress of *Concilium* (Brussels, 1970) did mark a new stage in development, but the effects only became apparent in 1972. We can, therefore, turn back to those seven years to inquire in what way the programme announced was in fact filled. Some points were better covered then than subsequently, for example ecumenical openings and writings by laity and non-believers. Some sections had to be abandoned for reasons quite independent of the inclinations of those responsible for the review: birth control was a subject of wide debate in the first issues, but it has never been examined in the review since because of Pope Paul's *Humanae Vitae* (1968). The problems examined, however, are certainly those facing the Church—or at least the Western churches; the methods used are certainly those announced; which made the most of the Moral Theology of the time. One thing is, however, worth observing: just as the themes relate, above all, to the questions facing the Western churches, so the authors are almost exclusively (87 per cent) from Western Europe; to be even more exclusive they are mostly Dutch or Germanic (this applies to thirty-nine contributions out of a total of sixty-six, i.e., 60 per cent, in the seven issues). It is true that in these two zones Moral Theology was of remarkable quality, showing great evidence of breadth of mind and awareness of the ways in which the problems surfaced elsewhere, but there was certainly some lack of balance.

The Congress of *Concilium* (Brussels, 1970) was bound to be of important consequence for the moral theology section. This was undoubtedly because for the first time the members of the editorial committee, residents of different countries and even different continents, first worked together 'in flesh and blood' and not by correspondence. At this congress, which was indeed international in character, they became involved in a vast interchange of ideas. Franz Böckle, still editor of the section on morality, claims to have been influenced: 'We very soon agreed that any attempt to substantiate ethical standards for people in our society has to take into account a very much altered and diversified form of self-awareness. Some typical aspects of this new self-consciousness are described in this issue, and some consideration is given to the problems which the situation poses for theological ethics.'[2]

The theme of this issue was, in fact, 'Man in a New Society'. However, the editor adds a most important methodological point, which is even more noteworthy to the reader familiar with the systematic nature of Germanic theology. 'Of course the magnitude of this theme made clear from the start that the present deliberations would be more a series of indications and stimuli than a comprehensive analysis.'[3] He also stresses further on in the editorial the remarks of the sociologist Wolf Lepenies, author of the opening article of that issue. Lepenies 'believes that the task of theology lies not so much in the working out of a unified ethics as in the establishment of criteria for the compatibility of diverse moral systems'.[4] Franz Böckle adds 'in this regard we may certainly say that . . . theology opens up the possibility of a plurality of actual expressions of morality. Nevertheless, any compatibility of the various projects must be clearly distinguished from wholly arbitrary choice . . . it (theology) must of course comply with the change in human self-understanding—as this is made apparent to the theologians from without',[5] assuming that this contribution is not uniform and monolithic, but plural and varied.

An examination of the issues published after this editorial shows that this editorial was, indeed, prophetic. The acknowledgement of diversity within theology is reflected in the variety of authors. Sixty-three per cent of these are Western European as opposed to the 87 per cent of the preceding period (this percentage was still too high but fell to 51 per cent for 1981-84). The number of Dutch and Germanic authors fell from 60 per cent to 30 per cent (25 per cent for 1981-84). A significant reversal is thus clearly evident. During and after the Council a fairly limited group of theologians, who had made significant contributions there, tried to extend their remarkable effort to the various local churches, where previously their attempt had had no hearing. The movement was centrifugal—as had been the former Roman theology! The aim was to extend the theology of the Council, hence the very name of the review, *Concilium*. Some years after the Council, however, these theologians stated, clearly and courageously, that the widest variety possible of theological research and human experience should be assembled, from every horizon, and put in communication and communion (this, in fact, was much closer to the very concept of Council). Instead of moving from the centre, the movement was directed towards the centre, or, to be more precise, the centre believed itself responsible for the establishment of reciprocal relations between the different communities. Within the last five years there have been five contributions from Asia (as opposed to none previously), three from Africa (none previously) and fourteen from Latin America (two previously). There has also been an increase in the number of woman writers, six over the last five years as opposed to three over fourteen years (all three figured in one issue: *Sexual Morality*).

Recognition of this need for variety was not restricted to the authors alone; it also concerned the problems faced and the methods adopted. The title of the 1972 issue, *Man in a New Society*, could apply generally to all the subsequent issues, especially if one were to define the different variations: the Christian in a new society, faith in a new society, the Christian in a new Church, etc. Subjects pertaining to fundamental morality were still treated: 'to discern the values in order to establish the morality' (No. 120 of the non-English language editions, 1976). The very use of the word 'discern', however, clearly indicates that the process tended to be exploratory rather than peremptory in character, and the same applies to the issue on moral formation (110, 1977). In one way or another, the problem of ethical plurality forms the subject matter of two issues: *Christian Ethics: Uniformity, Universality, Pluralism* (150, 1981) and *The Ethics of Liberation—The Liberation of Ethics* (172, 1984). One is made aware of certain splits within the Church and outside it (*The Dignity of the Despised of the Earth*, 130, 1977). The aim of the issue on *Sexual Morality* was not to impose an *a priori* theology on the subject but to make the reader aware of the multiform character of *The General Representation of Sexual Morality in Contemporary Catholicism* (this was the exact title of 100, 1974—in the non-English language editions).

The problems facing Christians, and humankind in general, have by no means lost their authenticity; but it is interesting, and reassuring, to note that they tend to reflect the changes in circumstances. During the 1970s, the Western world passed from rapid economic development to no development, and then to crisis. Between 1973 and 1975, the crisis was not yet very obvious (especially when one considers that the themes for the issues are determined almost two years before the date of publication); thus, the topics of discussion were ones like *Power and the Word of God* (90, 1973), *Sexuality in Contemporary Catholicism* (100, 1974) and *The Quality of Life* (101, 1975—in the non-English language editions). However, international or internal turmoils intensified at the same time as the economic crisis, hence one article on 'The Death Penalty and Torture' (120, 1978), a harrowing theme which unfortunately applies still to our time. Two other issues covered *Christian Ethics and Economics: The North-South Conflict* (140, 1980) and *Unemployment and the Right to Work* (160, 1982). Both these themes also apply, distressingly, to the present day.

As one of the two co-directors of the Moral Theology section since 1973 (working with Franz Böckle until 1978, and with Dietmar Mieth since then), I am in a very poor position to judge the quality of our work, although I am a warm supporter of the developments just summarised. I do feel, however, a certain dissatisfaction at our work, which concerns both the very essence of Christianity and a fundamental difficulty in Moral Theology. Max Weber distinguishes between the ethics of conviction and the ethics of responsibility. The greatness—and the difficulty—of the Christian ethic (more so than in all other ethics) lies in the fact that it must be both an ethic of conviction and an ethic of responsibility. The Christian ethic will always find its source and measure in a morality of conviction, the reason being in one name, or rather one person, Jesus Christ. But as the Christian ethic (much more so than all other ethics) claims to provide strength and light to communities and individuals in the most concrete structuring of their life, of their conduct and their institutions, the Christian ethic must be an ethic of responsibility. How can an ethic be simultaneously an ethic of conviction and responsibility? The paradox is virtually insoluble and it is hardly surprising that we have made little progress in this area; but I cannot help deploring the very limited nature of our success with it. A whole series of different mediations is required for our transition from the evangelical cry of protest, blessing . . . and cursing to a concrete morality which is truly developed and clearly defined. These mediations call in turn for the greatest variety of theoretical knowledge; they also require that acute attention be paid to the practices of both past and present. In my opinion our evangelical cry has sometimes been rather feeble, we have sometimes hardly succeeded in developing even the elements of a concrete morality, and we have sometimes got bogged down in the mediations that are meant to enable us to pass from one to the other simply because our theoretical knowledge was not sufficiently wide or diverse, and the attention we paid to the practices, old and new, was not sufficiently acute or open.

I will make no predictions about the future of the Moral Theology section in *Concilium*. Past experience has shown that the actual facts unfailingly belie such predictions. Who in 1960 could have foretold the point that Moral Theology would reach by Vatican II, as testified by Mgr Delhaye? Who, during the first few years of *Concilium*, could have predicted the extent and manner of its subsequent transformation? And who can predict now the tasks in store for moral theologians within the next five years, provided by the successes and failures of mankind in general and believers in particular, along with the inspiration of the Holy Spirit? While I myself make no such predictions, I must express a hope, and even a request, that in our Moral Theology section everything possible be done in order to develop an ethic of plurality (become *catholic* in the original meaning of the word) and communion (in another meaning of *catholic*) and an ethic of both conviction and responsibility. Let us be fervent in our fidelity to the prophetic character of Jesus of Nazareth; let us be more effective in our concern to come as close as possible to the formation of communities and persons by means of a truly concrete morality; finally, in order to pass more easily from one to the other, let our theoretical knowledge be more profound and varied, and let us be more attentive and open to what is actually done in practice. This is what is essential for good Moral Theology—no more, but certainly no less.

Translated by Patricia M. Newton

Notes

1. Philippe Delhaye 'The Contribution of Vatican II to Moral Theology' *Concilium* 75 (1972) p. 60.
2. Franz Böckle 'Editorial' *Concilium* 75 (1972) p. 7.
3. *Ibid.* p. 7.
4. *Ibid.* pp. 7-8.
5. *Ibid.* p. 8.

Giuseppe Alberigo

History and Theology: An Open Challenge

ONE OF the main ideas underlying the initial launch of *Concilium* was the inclusion of the historical dimension in the sphere that the new theological review identified as proper to its aims.[1] It was realised that this was a more significant development than a simple recognition of the fact that theological faculties at the time, as well as seminaries, placed the study of Church History formally (and often only formally) on the same level as that of classical theology.

Learned journals tended to stick closely to their own discipline, and communication between one and another was often virtually impossible. So Church History had a number of learned reviews devoted to it alone. *Concilium*'s novelty was to be inter-disciplinary, including an annual issue devoted to Church History as one of the ten, alongside Dogma, Liturgy, Pastoral problems, Ecumenism, Moral Theology, Church and World, Canon Law, Spirituality and Scripture. It thereby sought to state editorially that it regarded the study of history as being of equal academic importance with those other disciplines for forming a view on Christianity and the Church.

Born of experience during the Council of how the different disciplines could complement each other in approaching questions of Christian experience, this view had solid and well-established roots. Debate on the 'historicity' of Christianity had become widespread in the first decade of this century, and this led to debate on the legitimacy and value of a historical approach to Christianity itself. The debate hinged on the application of historico-critical methods to the study of the Old and New Testaments, reaching its most intense and dramatic phase in the Modernist controversy of the first decade of the century.[2] The harsh, intransigent polemics of that period had the effect of muddying and stultifying the whole debate, so that it could only be taken up again gradually and by a new generation, after the First World War.

Between the wars, European theology enjoyed a springtime, thanks in the main to its efforts at moving beyond the current 'baroque theology'—counter-reformationist, schematic, deductive and a-historical.[3]

It achieved this largely by a re-evaluation of the historical dimension of Christianity, following the lead given earlier by Newman and Möhler. This springtime was grounded on adequate and appropriate academic principles, urging the importance of method in theology, of going back to original sources, of the centrality of the biblical data of revelation. But it also had an ecclesial dimension, in so far as the liturgical, biblical and

66

ecumenical movements nourished themselves from the theological renewal and at the same time ensured that it retained vital contact with Christian experience.

The dramatic events of the Second World War on the one hand, and the growing timidity of Pius XII and his advisers in the face of demands for renewal on the other, backed up by the conviction on the part of 'Roman theology' that it alone was the repository of orthodox teaching, slowed down the diffusion and acceptance of renewal. The encyclical *Humani Generis* and the disciplinary sanctions that followed it were intended to nip in the bud any basic tendency to historicise theological investigation. This tendency was not to study the history of Christianity, of the Church, of theology, for their own sake, but to treat knowledge of the past as capable of throwing light on Christian thinking of the present. So the major facet of this new outlook was its recognition of the need to view Christianity itself in historical terms, and so its ecclesial existence, theological teaching and interaction with culture and society in the same light. This implied a rejection of the 'essentialist' concept of Christianity, the view of the Church as a society sufficient unto itself, and a pessimistic valuation of history, seen from outside, as it were, as a corrupt alternative to eternity.

So human history, and particularly the evolution of the Christian event in history, took on the dimension of a *'locus theologicus'*,[4] within which the 'signs of the times' called on intelligence illumined by faith to discern the traces of the kingdom that is to come. So the historicity that constituted Christian reality was rediscovered. From Marie-Dominique Chenu and Henri de Lubac to Teilhard de Chardin, many of the most astute minds engaged in reflection on Christianity moved in this direction, bringing about a substantial modification in the way in which theology was understood and in critical-rational understanding of Christianity itself.

As is well known, the announcement and then the holding of the second Vatican Council, and equally the whole pontificate of John XXIII, brought about a substantially different climate, which consisted largely in recognition of the importance of the historical dimension, which John XXIII's own cultural background and theological bent made him particularly aware of.[5] It is not by chance that the most significant elements in the teaching of Vatican II relate to the intrinsic historicity of the Church, borne out most evidently in the second chapter of *Lumen Gentium*, on the people of God, the historical condition in which Christianity and Christians live, re-emphasised in the Pastoral Constitution of the Church in the modern world, which marked the Church's exit from the secular condition of 'Christendom' as symbiotic with Western culture, and in the new consciousness of living in a new phase of human existence which inspired the Decree on Missionary Activity.[6]

Other fundamental decisions, such as the sovereignty of the Word of God, the absolute call to ecumenical effort and the need for liturgical reform were also basically inspired by the conviction of being a Church on pilgrimage through history, on its way to the kingdom. This conviction also led the Council to reiterate the importance of Church History as a subject for study and research.[7]

This insistence enables one to understand what lay behind the basic intentions of *Concilium* as set out by Karl Rahner and Edward Schillebeeckx in their 'General Introduction', when they stated that *Concilium* 'has chosen to pursue a definite direction—the direction indicated by Vatican II'.[8] As I have already said, this resulted in one of the ten issues in every year being devoted to Church History, with Roger Aubert as Editor and Anton Weiler as Assistant Editor.[9] This gives a new dimension to the Review, involving as it did some twenty qualified Church historians as Associate Editors, involved in the preparation of each Church History issue, and interdisciplinary contact between those responsible for this section of the Review and the editors of the other nine, through the annual meetings of the Board of Editorial Directors.

This underlying impetus in fact produced, from 1965 to 1972, an interesting, fruitful and significant result in the shape of eight issues devoted to Church History. These in turn were divided into the first two, made up of articles on varied topics, and the next six, each devoted to a particular theme. As always, the non-monographic presentation of the first two issues enabled a wide variety of subjects to be tackled, giving the reader a broad spectrum of information, ideas for new lines of research, renewed understanding of historical problems of particular complexity and importance.

The presence of historical contributions was not limited to the issues devoted to Church History. The early issues of *Concilium* frequently contained historical articles, usually thorough surveys of the evolution of a particular problem or of an institution through the course of Christian history.

Overall, those two years when historical studies were an integral part of a great theological Review have left a favourable impression, though some doubts remain. The articles that appeared were free from any residue of apologetics, and of a high critical and methodological standard. The problems treated were dealt with at a level that would not have disgraced any of the international historical journals, though the nature of *Concilium* did not lend itself to the publication of basic analytical research or the edition of original texts.

In 1967 the Executive Editorial Committee decided that all issues of the Review should adopt the 'monograph' formula, each issue being devoted to one aspect of the discipline to which each section of the Review corresponded. This decision often produced issues of great significance, but at the same time it drastically reduced the possibility of including timely items of information or guidance on current problems.

So from 1967 to 1972 there appeared a series of issues each dealing either with one significant aspect of Christian Experience: *Christianity and Culture* (1967), *Prophecy* (1968), *Sacralisation and Secularisation* (1969), *Election-Consensus-Reception* (1972), or with subjects of methodology, such as the relationship between the Church and science (1970) or the nature of Church History as the way the Church understands itself (1971).

Each of these subjects was certainly treated at a high level, produced interesting issues and performed a real service for the readers. In some cases individual articles provided the reference point and set the tone for international discussion of a topic for years to come.[10] On the other hand, one cannot completely escape the impression of a certain tiredness creeping into the efforts to achieve a truly dialectical and fruitful relationship with the other disciplines represented in *Concilium*. Despite the best endeavours, the impression is of parallelism rather than of effective integration.

The most significant expression given to this problem was in the 1971 issue, dealing precisely with the historical consciousness of Christianity as the way in which the Church understands itself.[11] This issue dealt at length with the outstanding contribution history can make to understanding the Christian experience from within, as an essentially historical reality, at least in the dimension accessible to human reason.

This issue proposed the possibility of a reading of Christianity not only in the perspective of salvation and the divine plan that underlies it, but also on a positive plane, precisely, that is, through the rigorous application of historico-critical methods. Such an endeavour gives special point to the aim set out as early as the first Editorial in 1965, that Church history should not concern itself just with isolated events, personages and doctrines, but with a reading of the whole of Christianity as an event which defines itself as historical.

This complex *prise de conscience* raised many thorny problems in relation to traditionally theological disciplines on the one hand, and with the affirmation—dear to several contemporary schols of thought—of the theandric nature of the Church, on the other.

The beginning of the 1970s saw a hardening of positions on whether the history of the

Church should have a place among theological disciplines.[12] Clearly those who propose the wholly critical-positivist, non-theological status of Church History have to re-think its relationship to the theological disciplines, a problem which has traditionally been resolved empirically and on the quiet by making Church History on principle a branch of theology, a relationship seen in practice as one of marginality and subordination. Another aspect of the matter was that the happy and fruitful integration of various disciplines during Vatican II, when historians and theologians got along so well with each other, proved difficult to sustain outside the exceptional atmosphere of the Council.

All these considerations influenced the 1971 decision, implemented in 1973, to consider the Church History section (along with the Scripture one), a sort of basic section, with the implication that it would no longer have a separate issue each year but should be considered to be present as a basic dimension in all sections of *Concilium*.[13] To this end the Editor and Assistant Editor continued as members of the Board of Editorial Directors even though they no longer had specific issues to prepare.

This was an interesting concept, though not without its dangers; its results can be seen in the issues of the next ten years (1973-82). As far as the number of historical articles go, this has varied with the disciplines: there have been most in the issues devoted to Church Institutions and Spirituality, fewest and most insignificant in Practical Theology and Sociology of Religion. There has not been a year in which all sections have included at least one historical article, nor has any of the sections included at least one in all its ten issues. This is not in fact very different from 1965-66 when, even though there was a section specifically devoted to Church History, the other issues also included historical articles. But perhaps more interesting than numbers of articles is the cultural impact of the historical pieces that have appeared, seen as a contribution to each single-subject issues and the overall impression given by the Review.

The historical pieces have generally appeared at the front of each issue, designed to give readers some idea of how the subject under review was dealt with in the past, generally in the first centuries of the Church. They have also, less frequently, been descriptions of the diacronic evolution of a particular issue over a long period, thereby helping to distinguish its permanent elements from its more recent ones. Occasionally, articles on a particular historical episode have appeared, generally shedding little light on the topic under review and so diminishing the usefulness of that issue.

The overall structure of each issue has tended to fall into two camps. Topics are often treated from strictly present-day points of view, phenomenonically as well as doctrinally, with no account taken of the historical aspects of the subjects (its history, the history of how it has been dealt with, the historical context in which it is set). At other times the structure has envisaged one article (rarely more) of a historical-retrospective nature, designed to give background information without really adding anything new to the topic under discussion. Apart from some exceptional cases, this appears to be the 'basic' role assigned to Church History. While the intention was to give expression to the potentially fruitful insight, in reality this has proved somewhat elusive, the result being a certain number of historical articles almost always of marginal relevance and subsidiary to the central points of the subject of that issue. These articles have furthermore inevitably been lacking in critical incisiveness, despite the high level of erudition they display. This is generally because the writer has been offered only a marginal space in the issue, which has excluded him from the basic debate being conducted in that issue, and had his contribution thereby limited to that of a purveyor of straightforward information.

In view of this state of affairs, it seems legitimate to ask what has caused such an obvious gap between the original intention stated in 1965 and restated in 1971 on the one hand, and the picture that has in fact emerged since then, on the other.

Part of the explanation would seem to come from a comparison with ten other theological reviews.[14] A glance at the last ten years' issues of these would show that all of them have over the past ten years devoted very little space to historical contributions, on average far less that *Concilium*. They also show that any integration between historical and theological research has been episodic at best, though it must be said that the historical articles in these reviews, being unfettered by a monographic concept, usually possess a greater critical incisiveness than those in *Concilium*, being the fruit of original research rather than limited to giving information. This original dimension has usually been lacking in *Concilium*, with the result that, with a few exceptions, the issues have been deprived of something that had been considered fundamental to them.

Going beyond comparisons, it has to be said that the elimination from *Concilium* of a section devoted solely to the history of Christianity has proved an insuperable obstacle to any chance of its being a vehicle for airing the major questions thrown up by research into the history of religion. The most recent trends in historiography, such as the importance given to long-term phenomena, the emphasis on oral sources and 'material' culture—to give only two examples out of a whole host—have been excluded, despite their particular relevance and fruitfulness for the understanding of Christian life. The same goes for attempts at an overall understanding of the Christian event outside its sectional components—teaching, preaching, piety, institutions, etc.—or confessional ones.

These remarks could also apply the other way round, in the sense that an osmosis of theological research in its dealings with the history of the church has also been lacking. It has often happened that profound modifications of central dogmatic elements, of ecclesiology or of the relationship between Church and society have been made without reference to the historians or to their way of working on the history of the Church.

The last and perhaps deepest level of explanation is to be found in the great changes that have taken place in the general culture and spiritual climate over the past ten years. The great shock given to European and North American culture in 1968 brought a radical critique of historical understanding as one of its major consequences, leading to a rejection of the past by the younger generation, who felt it to be an unjustifiable weight and imposition on the present and future. This confrontation was not devoid of basis or positive results, but at the same time it left a residual unease and sometimes a sense of guilt the traces of which can be found in a weakening of the cultural identity of certain sectors of society, or in a diffidence towards study of the past, seeing in it only the purpose of acquiring knowledge of a time that is shut off from us and therefore of only archaeological interest. I believe this crisis has had its repercussions on the status of Church History in *Concilium* over the past decade.

Perhaps of more immediate relevance, however, has been the growing distance in time from the experience of Vatican II, when close collaboration between historians and theologians had proved not only necessary but capable of producing significant results. The existence of a common aim—collaboration in the work of the Council—had provided a specific incentive and a stimulating occasion for inter-disciplinary convergence.[15] In the post-conciliar years this stimulus has gradually become more feeble, and despite the sincere intentions underlying the launching of *Concilium*, it has proved increasingly difficult to recognise a common motivation. This has meant that the division of the Review into sections basically corresponding to the traditional disciplines taught in the ecclesiastical institutions has become rather a centrifugal force, emphasising the specificity of each discipline instead of common aims and reasons for coming together.

The major development of the years since the Council has, however, been the increase in Christian thought in areas where Christianity is not the basic culture, which used simply to copy Western theology. So there has been renewed contact with Eastern theology of the Orthodox tradition on one hand, and a dawning of Christian thought uncovering the fruitful relationship between the Gospel and the great, long-subordinated cultures of Latin America, Africa and large parts of Asia on the other. This has produced a thrust towards a significant 'regionalisation' of Christian thought itself and so of Church history. Slowly and with difficulty, a new way of looking at and constructing the history of the Christian experience is being born, taking account of the cultural specificity of different areas, trying to understand its own Christian past set on the soil from which its own people sprang, rather than on missionary importations.[16] This way of looking at the past so as to build one's own identity from it is a new challenge to all organs of historical and theological research, and still more to *Concilium*.

Just because the intuition born during Vatican II gave rise to such a novel undertaking as *Concilium*, which has been a significant force for renewal, so it is legitimate now to stress the need for a new effort to take another leap forward and take up the new challenge. Today the obvious reason for coming together and bringing Christian thinking into a common endeavour is to be found in Christian experience itself, within which the old distinctions between disciplines are seen to be less and less relevant. A Christian experience which is historical by its nature cannot be adequately understood without historical investigation being a habitual dimension in all thinking, not just a process of providing information about a past which we think we have overcome but which nevertheless conditions and helps to determine our present and our future.

Translated by Paul Burns

Notes

1. K. Rahner and E. Schillebeeckx 'General Introduction' Vol. I, No. 1 (1965) p. 3.
2. See *La Crise contemporaine du Modernisme à la crise des hermeneutiques* (Paris 1973).
3. The learned 'manifesto' was *Le Saulchoir. Une école de théologie*, edited by M.-D. Chenu and distributed in 1937, but placed on the Index in 1942. See my Introduction to the Italian edition, *Christianesimo come storia e teologia* (Casale Monferrato 1982).
4. Y. Congar 'Church History as a Branch of Theology' 57 (1970) p. 85.
5. See the opening discourse of Vatican II of 11 October 1962, in AAS 54, pp. 786-795.
6. A quick reading is enough to show the frequency and incisiveness with which the documents of Vatican II use terms such as *aetas, aevum, historia, hodie, tempus*. Such language is almost completely absent from the documents of Vatican I.
7. UR 5; OT 16, GS 54.
8. p. 8.
9. See their Editorial in *Concilium* Vol. 7, No. 1 (1965) p. 3.
10. I would like to remind everyone of the article by Y. Congar on reception as an ecclesiological reality, in *Concilium* 77 (1972) p. 43.
11. See the Editorial to 57 (1971) by A. Weiler.
12. See the long work by H. R. Seeliger *Kirchengeschichte-Geschichtstheologie-Geschichtswissenschaft. Analysen zur Wissenschafttheorie und Theologie der katholischen Kirchengeschichtsschreibung* (Düsseldorf 1981).
13. This was to be part of the 'new force' of *Concilium*, referred to in 80 (1972) at p. 16.
14. *Journal of Theological Studies* (Oxford); *Revue des Sciences philosophiques et théologiques* (Paris); *Revue théologique de Louvain; Theological Studies* (Baltimore); *Theologie und Philosophie* (Frankfurt); *Theologische Quartalschrift* (Tübingen); *Tijdschrift voor Theologie* (Nijmegen); *Zeitschrift für katholische Theologie* (Vienna).

F

15. See the account given by M.-D. Chenu in 'Theology as an Ecclesial Science' in *Concilium* Vol. 1, No. 3 (1967) at p. 47.

16. The most recent evidence of this comes from the meeting that took place in Basle from 12 to 17 October 1981, under the heading 'Church History in an Ecumenical Perspective', where many historians from Latin America, Africa, Asia and Oceania took part. The proceedings were published in a special issue of the *Theologische Zeitschrift* 38 (1972) pp. 257-492.

Bas van Iersel

Exegesis: The First and the Second Decades and the Future

IN MOST of the editions of *Concilium*, No. 10, the last issue of the year in the case of this international journal, was originally devoted to exegesis. In many systems of points, ten is the highest possible number. Because the highest number is so seldom reached, however, no one would ever have imagined that ten in this case expressed the supreme status of exegesis. Certainly the editors of this section never saw it in that light. For them, ten was simply the order of appearance: exegesis was the tenth and last theological discipline to appear each year. The reason for its appearing last was very simple: it was originally the last section to be manned and was in fact fully manned only when the preparations for the first year (1965) were well under way. I was involved in those initial preparations and I am still very glad, even now, that the speed with which those plans had to be made did not result in the section having to make do with a second choice of editors. The very opposite was true: in P. Benoit (Jerusalem) and R. Murphy (who was at that time in Washington), exegesis had two directors who were more than merely competent both in their own specialised sphere and in the general management of the journal. The journal undoubtedly benefited a great deal not only from the international reputation, but also from the confidence that they enjoyed and still enjoy throughout the world.

The history of the exegetical section can be divided into two phases. Although we cannot divide that history precisely into two periods of exactly ten years each, it is convenient to call the earlier phase the 'first decade' and the more recent one the 'second decade'. I will discuss each of these stages in turn in this article and then say something about the 'future' of the section, by which I do not, of course, mean the very distant future.

1. THE FIRST DECADE

The first phase, which is not a complete decade, was from 1965 to 1973 and in those years exegesis was number ten. During the first three years of its existence, *Concilium* had no section title on the cover and the reader could only find out what the central theme was from the editorial. The editors believed that it was valueless to repeat in the exegetical issues what was already being done in journals specialising in exegesis. The

73

material provided by *Concilium* had to fit into the framework of a theological journal and had to be treated in such a way that readers who were not trained in exegesis could also understand the articles.

It was partly because of this that the nature and function of Holy Scripture itself were considered in the first years of *Concilium*. In the first issue (1965), Scripture was discussed as the book of the people of God, with the emphasis on the people. The articles were concerned with inspiration and revelation, the importance of the history of the origin of the Old and New Testaments, the canon and the function of Scripture and its use in the Church's preaching. In addition to these more general considerations, there were also several studies devoted to biblical theology and exegesis: the Torah of Moses and Christ the Redeemer; Jesus, the first and last Word of God (Mark 1:1-13; John 2:1-18) and the people of God according to Eph. 1:3-14. The number also included a bulletin on the prophetic literature and one on the Wisdom literature. I have dealt in some detail with the contents of this first issue, because the exegetical issues during the first decade followed this pattern fairly closely. They consisted, in other words, of a number of general considerations of a theme with the addition of articles on biblical theology and textual analysis. The latter may have been quite closely related to the theme of the particular issue, but they were still a comparatively arbitrary choice made from many possibilities.

The first issue was based on the belief that the Scriptures had been the products of a community of believers. The second issue (1966) had as its theme the dynamism of the biblical tradition. This was a more specific theme, with the result that the impression made by this issue is more uneven than that made by the first. I will return to this question later, but now we must turn to the third issue (1967), which was more explicit than the previous two issues directed at the reader of Scripture or the reading community. Its theme was the value of the Old Testament for the Christian community of faith. The bulletins at the end of this third issue were concerned with the many different meanings of Scripture and its function in various other religious communities. The three following issues dealt with themes that were explicitly related to biblical theology: the Eucharist (1968), the presence and the absence of God (1969) and immortality and resurrection (1970).

The quality of these early numbers was uneven, partly because it was often quite difficult to persuade the authors whom the editors had approached as first choice to co-operate. The reason for this was obvious. The editors planned an issue and then asked the authors who seemed best to fit in with that plan to write an article. The most important authors sometimes found this troublesome, because they did not like editors to prescribe the outcome of their studies. The editors understood their problem very well, but could not see their way to changing this situation. The problem was one which was very characteristic of the situation in which the planners and those carrying out the plan had different ideas.

From the seventh issue of *Concilium* onwards, the way of working was more interdisciplinary. The theme in 1971 was theology, exegesis and proclamation. In three of the contributions, an exegete and a dogmatic theologian collaborated. This was an interesting experiment and brought to light both the possibilities and the problems of such a collaboration. The last contribution to the exegetical section was again a matter of biblical theology and dealt with offices in the Church (1972). The biblical data were treated within the framework of the question of finding solutions to the problem of office in the Church, which had in the meantime become quite acute. This issue was the most interdisciplinary to date in the exegetical section of the journal and was therefore an obvious transition from the first decade to the new pattern that began to emerge in the second decade in 1973.

This marked the end of the editorial collaboration of the first decade. The great distances caused by the triangle Jerusalem-Washington-Nijmegen had often made it difficult for the editors to work together, but they had been helped by the advisory committee, some of the members of which are professional colleagues who have continued on the committee from 1965 until the present. These include Luis Alonso Schökel, Jacques Dupont, Lucas Grollenberg, Herbert Haag, Franz Mussner, Rudolf Schnackenburg, Heinz Schürmann, David Stanley, Francis Bruce Vawter (who also served for a number of years as one of the two editors-in-chief) and Anton Vögtle. Almost all of them have at one time or another made contributions to *Concilium*. About seventy people have collaborated in one way or another in the issues in the exegetical section.

What are the most striking aspects of the eight exegetical issues that were published during the first phase? The most positive feature is, I think, that they were more easily understandable than most of the other issues. Articles that were difficult to understand have been exceptional and whenever the editors received an article written in difficult language, they have not hesitated to describe it as such. Leaving aside the last issue in this early phase of *Concilium*'s existence, I can only describe a second aspect of the exegetical issues paradoxically by saying that they were striking because they were in a sense not striking. Exegetes were perhaps less conscious of the renewal that followed the Second Vatican Council than other theologians. Or were they at that time just living in a period between the renewal of the literary and historical method and what followed it? Whatever the case may be, if *Concilium* was then, as it is now, the mouthpiece of loyal opposition to the theology of the manuals, the exegetical issues expressed both loyalty and opposition.

The exegetical issues were also unexciting and even flat. This may have been because it was difficult to link them directly to the burning questions of the period and because a journal such as *Concilium* was not the right vehicle for the propagation of new exegetical ideas. The 1972 issue on offices in the Church was an exception to this general pattern of calmly imparting information. The theme was very contemporary and urgent at the time and even now, more than a decade later, we are no nearer to a solution of the problem. The urgency of the problem in 1972 can be seen from the remarkable fact that there was an exegetical article about the same subject in an issue not devoted to exegesis in the same year and another exegetical article in another non-exegetical issue shortly afterwards. This is the only case, as far as I know, of the contents being, as it were, repeated in the field of exegesis in the journal.

2. THE SECOND DECADE

The specifically exegetical issues of *Concilium* ceased in 1973, when *Concilium* was given a new face. The intention was that exegetes should collaborate regularly in the production of issues on certain themes in the other sections and that every effort should be made to make the journal interdisciplinary. Has this aim been achieved? The results can be seen by comparing the two phases in the history of *Concilium*. There were altogether seventeen contributions by exegetes in the seventy-two issues that were not exegetical and were published up to 1973.[1] I have looked through 108 contributions in the second period and fifty-three of these have been exegetical. During the same period, these exegetical contributions have also been spread more widely and in a different way in the issues of the various sections. In the first decade, most of the exegetical articles can be found in the issues devoted to dogmatic, pastoral, moral and ecumenical theology. There is a striking absence of such articles in the issues dealing with fundamental theology.

What is the explanation for this? I think it is to be found in the nature of the themes discussed in these issues. Most of the exegetical studies in the second decade of the publication of *Concilium* appear in the dogmatic, ecumenical and liturgical sections. Far fewer can be found in the sections devoted to spirituality, moral theology, religious sociology and fundamental theology. I do not think that an attempt to find out whether these very divergent exegetical contributions made to different issues of *Concilium* point in a similar direction or express a similar view would be very valuable, but I do think that it is worth observing that they are written at a high level, as they were during the first decade, and that they are not difficult to understand.

What is, I believe, really valuable in this context is to look back critically at the decision leading to the cessation of the specifically exegetical issues. In the first place, I am bound to say quite explicitly that this decision was taken as early as 1971, that it was based on very good motives and that it was unanimous. This means, of course, that I was also in agreement with it. I have to say now, however, that it was taken at an exceptionally unfortunate time.

It was unfortunate, because it was taken on the eve of the breakthrough of new developments in exegesis. Until then, the 'official' science of exegesis had been almost exclusively practised within the framework of the literary and historical method, the components of which were the history of traditions, form criticism and redactio-historical studies. Alongside this main current there were no more than a few little streams, one of which was, for example, the existential and psycho-analytical interpretation. There was a great increase in criticism between 1960 and 1970, but no new models of research and interpretation emerged.

Between 1970 and 1980, however, the situation changed. The prevailing opinions in the field of exegesis were attacked. The buildings constructed by the literary and historical establishment did not collapse, but it became clear that new firms were in competition with it. It was just at that time that the decision was taken not to produce any more exegetical issues for *Concilium*, with the result that the journal was unable to keep its readers in touch with what was taking place in the world of exegesis.

It would be more true to say that it was almost unable to do this, since what the exegetical section could no longer do, the others could. In 1980, for example, the ecumenical section devoted an issue to the theme: the Bible and its interpretation. Following the formula normally applied in the ecumenical issues, of publishing many short articles written from different points of view, almost all the existing and new methods of research in exegesis were reviewed. These included the historico-critical method, two types of exegesis that are more orientated towards structuralism, the materialistic and the psycho-analytical interpretation of the Bible, Jewish exegesis, the type of interpretation made against the background of experiences in Brazilian basic communities, the position of South African negroes with regard to the Bible and the feminist view of Scripture. This was an excellent issue of its kind, but I wonder whether these new approaches were not dealt with too briefly, with the result that the reader could have no more than a superficial impression. The mere fact that this issue appeared, however, seems to me to be very significant: a specifically exegetical issue appearing in a different section without any contribution by an editor-in-chief and almost without the collaboration of the editorial committee.

This was certainly not the first or the last time that blood proved to be thicker than water. In 1975, there was a liturgical issue that at least approached the frontiers of exegesis in dealing with the theme of the Bible in the liturgy (1975, 2) and in 1983, the title of the issue on spirituality was *Job and the Silence of God* (1983, 9). As I write this article, I cannot, of course, know what that issue will be like. When it was being planned, it was made clear that the subject was not to be treated exegetically, but the rest of the plan certainly gave the impression that the non-exegetical approach was only true if the word 'exegesis' was understood in the narrow technical and professional sense. To judge from the original plan, the issue promises to be exceptionally interesting and very original. Professional exegetes would probably not have planned it in this way, but it would certainly not be out of place in an issue in the exegetical section.

These issues are also very significant, but to what do they in fact point? I think that they point to a real need for issues devoted to Scripture or at least a part of it. I feel bound to ask whether it would not be sensible to give some thought to the question as to whether the exegetical section could not be made fully productive again. They may possibly also point to the fact that theologians consciously or unconsciously reject any kind of monopoly on the part of exegetes in writing or that they believe that exegetes are too one-sidedly preoccupied with Scripture. Exegetes should think very seriously about this whole development and examine the diagnosis carefully before deciding whether therapy is required and, if so, what kind of therapy.

3. THE FUTURE?

In reflection, I decided to furnish this heading with a question mark. It is too early to tell whether the exegetical section will in future produce its own issues. If it does not, there is not much to be said about the future task of exegesis in *Concilium*. A kind of interim solution might perhaps be preferable.

Such an interim solution could be based on the twofold task of exegetes. On the one hand, professional exegesis is an ancillary science at the service of systematic theology. On the other hand, however, it has an independent function of its own. It does not require the mediation of other theologians and is directed at anyone who wishes to hear it, in particular at the community of believers who regard the reading of Scripture and its exegesis as necessary.

The present arrangement deals quite satisfactorily with the first aspect in that exegetes are asked regularly to make contributions to issues in other sections. We must expect those contributions in the foreseeable future to be based on the literary and historical method or on biblical theology or to be interpretations of parts of Scripture that are relevant to a particular theological theme.

It would, on the other hand, only be possible to deal satisfactorily with the second aspect of exegesis as an independent science if the section were able at least from time to time to produce an issue of its own. What should be the contents of these exegetical issues? There are several possibilities. I think, for example, that there is an urgent need for the new methods of reading, analysing and understanding Scripture to be elucidated and also for them to be seen in relationship to each other. In the specialised journals they have been so compartmentalised that their interrelationship has been almost completely ignored. The literary-historical method still predominates in the classical journals that have existed for some time. The other methods are exploited in certain journals both in the French and English and in the German linguistic zones.

Another very important possibility seems to me to be to contribute to what I would, for the time being, call the emancipation of non-professional readers of the Bible, who differ from each other in many ways, but who all share one thing in common with each other, namely that they do not study the Bible scientifically. They form in fact a kind of opposition to the official scientific study of the Bible. Those who do study the Bible as a science should certainly not rest content with their task. On the contrary, they should accept as a second task, alongside their primary scientific task, the advancement of that emancipation. That task cannot or can hardly be performed with the framework of the existing scientific journals specialising in biblical studies, but it might well be a suitable function for the exegetical section of *Concilium*, especially if a specifically exegetical issue could be published from time to time. It might also possibly lead to the editorial committee being reinforced with exegetes who are particularly active in this sphere. That is something that could be achieved without very much trouble.

Translated by David Smith

Note

1. I was able to trace the exegetical contributions made to the non-exegetical issues during the years preceding 1973 with the help of the general index provided by the Spanish publisher of *Concilium*, Ediciones Cristianidad of Madrid, one of the members of the team at the beginning who produced the first eight volumes of the journal. The data for the period from 1973 to the present were provided by Sr Hadewych Snijdewind of the Secretariat in Nijmegen. Both have saved me a great deal of time and I am deeply indebted to them.

Odilo Metzler

'Third World' Theology in *Concilium*

IN THIS article we shall be taking a look at some of the new approaches in theology in 'Third World' countries which have been published in this journal. The main emphasis is on the Latin-American contributions in the area of liberation theology, which have had a formative influence on *Concilium*. This is complemented by new and often markedly contrasting approaches in the theology coming from Africa and Asia. We cannot analyse all the 120 monographs which have appeared since 1973; what is presented is an initial impression of significant trends in 'regional' theology.*

LATIN-AMERICAN LIBERATION THEOLOGY—A PROPHETIC THEOLOGY COMING FROM THE WORLD OF THE OPPRESSED

Even in the early 1960s the realisation of the increasing misery of the so-called 'Third World', together with the revolutionary ferment in the Latin-American sub-continent, resulted in a profound reorientation in the Church of Latin America. Bishops attacked the unjust structures and demanded wide reforms; whole groups of Christians pledged themselves to a social revolution. The Latin-American Synod of Bishops at Medellín (1968) spoke of the vicious circle of poverty as sin and of 'opting for the poor'. After a period in which social conditions were subjected to a prophetic and theological critique,[1] the 1970s saw much thorough reflection on theology's presuppositions, social locus and particular field of interest. Various theologians developed and pursued this budding theology of liberation.

What is common to this theology is that it takes as its starting-point the 'signs of the times', reality as it is; in order to recognise it not only personal experience but also technical analysis are necessary. Here it first of all employs the techniques of class analysis and the theory of dependence, which provide the key to an interpretation of the historical, political and socio-economic situation and its causes.

The picture of man presupposed in the analysis of society is characterised in liberation theology by the 'option for the poor', that is, taking the part of the disadvantaged masses as the expression of love for Christ in one's neighbour.

This 'opting for the poor' is not only a premiss in the analysis of reality and in theological reflection: it calls for intervention in the world of the oppressed and the exploited. Identification with their interests and struggles becomes the starting-point for a new way of being human and living out one's faith. This new way of historical existence and 'praxis', in which one refashions both history and oneself, leads to a new way of knowing.[2] Thus, being involved in the struggle for liberation, 'orthopraxis', becomes the locus of theological understanding. It transposes the Christian into a different culture and leads to a spirituality of liberation in which the politician and the mystic become one: in the peoples' cry for liberation faith hears the call of God.[3]

This theology sees itself as being critical of society, as being the second word to the first word spoken by the human and social sciences. With their help it understands that reality is deformed, and determines to transform it and liberate the oppressed. The deformation of reality is expressed in the refusal of the 'other', in fratricide, in the oppressive status quo. This refusal of the 'other' is the sin of the world, the original sin. It is reinforced by deifying itself, by refusing the creative Other, God. Thus the status quo becomes the most grievous rejection of the gift of divine governance, namely, structural sin.[4]

A divergence of opinion soon appeared with regard to theology's contribution to the struggle for liberation. Whereas H. Assmann saw the main task of theology and Christian praxis in a 'structural' decision on the part of faith in favour of the political option and had nothing to say about theology's critical or discerning function *vis-à-vis* concrete historical projects, Scannone pointed out the danger of a political manipulation of faith and of theology if the revolutionary option were absolutised as an ideology and liberation were simply equated with revolution. It is by no means clear, as he observed, that the revolutionary position is prepared, in its turn, to submit to questioning on the part of faith. S. Galilea was critical of the fact that, by adopting the Marxist analysis, a socio-political view had been presupposed which improperly restricted the meaning of commitment to liberation.[5]

This example shows the broad spectrum of approaches in liberation theology, from the strategic on the one hand to the critical on the other, aiming to keep the struggle for liberation open, in each historical situation and form, to the eschatological perspective.

They are united, of course, in the conviction that theological discourse must emerge from concrete liberation praxis and be validated by it. The truth of the Gospel is a truth to be *done*, a liberating truth with historical consequences. And as for the message to the poor, it will not be a liberating message until the poor themselves are those who carry it. Theology must draw upon them for its knowledge. In 'basic communities' they themselves learn how to be theological *subjects*, interpreting the Gospel anew in the light of their historical situation, and interpreting and remodelling their history in the light of the Gospel. History is thus to be overcome, to yield new faith-experience.

2. DISCIPLESHIP AND THE UTOPIA OF THE KINGDOM OF GOD

Liberation theology understands the repression and suffering of the people as the historical continuation of the suffering of the Suffering Servant of the Bible. This repression, and its accompanying yearning for liberation, have become signs of the times. Yet there is a danger here that such stress is laid on the fact of oppression (e.g., in El Salvador or Guatemala) that the horror of the cross itself is completely missed. The oppressed people believe in the Son of God because they are like him as the Suffering Servant. Jose Sobrino compares many Latin American people to the Suffering Servant in that they have no human face, no justice, they are maltreated and downtrodden. Like the Suffering Servant they try to introduce justice and righteousness; they fight for their liberation. In consequence, just like him, they are oppressed and persecuted. They know that they have been chosen for this role, that liberation is coming through them, and they interpret their own plight as the path to this liberation. They become like the Crucified in the experience of their own suffering. In their own pain and powerlessness they come to understand him, and in his cross they see themselves.

Elements of discipleship of the suffering Righteous One are to be seen in the way in which people take the part and share the fate of the humiliated, endeavouring in a spirit of love to liberate others in the hope of the coming Kingdom, and in the spirit of the Beatitudes, which reveals the very essence of Jesus.

On this basis Sobrino draws up a catalogue of virtues: 'This means that the followers of Jesus must always keep a spirit of mercy in their hearts in the midst of the struggle necessary to achieve justice; they must keep a clear eye open to God's truth: he does not trivialise the struggles of the oppressed by reducing them all to equal value, but judges them by what they can produce; they must work for peace, make the ideal of peace an ingredient in the struggle for justice, even though this struggle, however justly and even nobly undertaken, always involves some degree of violence, which in extreme cases can even include legitimate armed insurrection. They must above all be ready to face persecution, to bear themselves with fortitude in persecution, even to the point of giving their lives, a sign of the greatest love that man can have, and proof that following Jesus is really pro-existence.'[6]

An oppressed people's experience of God and relation to him is shown in the confidence it places in liberation and in its obedience in the service of liberation.

One form taken by the world's sin is unemployment, which, in the Third World, attains massive proportions, depriving three-quarters of the population of the fundamentals of existence. This sin of the world, this lack of solidarity, is inimical to the kingdom of God. In this situation the Third World demands conversion and change: not only the creation 'of a new world economic order in which relations of exchange are more just, but of a new civilisation which is no longer built upon the pillars of hegemony and domination, accumulation and difference, consumption and false well-being, but upon more human and Christian foundations'.[7]

Ellacuria states three maxims which are to govern a new world economic order and a new structure of relationships between peoples: (*a*) a human order, oriented to the Utopian ideal of the kingdom of God, is being initiated primarily by and for the poor; (*b*) it demands a change in the hierarchy of values: wealth, power, consumerism and egoism must be overcome, for they hinder the intelligent sharing of work and the revaluing of countless creative activities; and (*c*) an important principle is that of 'working for a civilisation of poverty, in which poverty would not be the deprivation of necessary and fundamental needs . . . [but] a universal state of things, in which the satisfaction of fundamental needs was guaranteed, and also the freedom of personal choice and an atmosphere of personal and communal creativity . . .'.[8]

3. NEW THEOLOGICAL APPROACHES IN ASIA

For the most part the situation of the Church in Asia is different from that in Latin America. Most of the Asian Churches are small in numbers, isolated from one another and obliged to struggle lest they disappear among the multitudes of adherents of the other religions or succumb to Communist domination. A large proportion of the articles from Asia are concerned with dialogue with their religious, political or cultural environment. Often—in India for instance—theology is faced with the urgent task of contributing to the process of inculturation. An interesting article by Duraisamy Amalorpavadass on 'The Poor with No Voice and No Power'[9] shows that, in doing so, it can come to conclusions similar to those of the Latin American liberation theology.

He compares the religious and cultural heritage of India to a river. One dives in and is carried along on one's search for *mokṣa* (redemption/liberation). The spirit of poverty is the expression of a contemplative life of unity with God, of detachment in order to serve higher goals. It presupposes material poverty and the willingness to share, i.e., to give away one's goods to those who are in need. Poverty without a cosmic dimension, a relation to the community and a spiritual experience, is therefore meaningless.

The social scene of India, as of the 'Third World', is characterised by the fact that, as a result of institutionalised oppression, 50 per cent of the population have to live in misery, below the subsistence level, as non-persons, as non-human beings. The Bible is quoted as theology's starting-point with regard to both these facets of reality. The biblical message, in the Beatitudes in Luke for instance, is primarily addressed to the poor, who are the victims of injustice and increasing poverty, and secondarily to all who are looking for God to change the situation. A total revolution has been set in motion on behalf of the poor, and it embraces the whole world. Its aim is to liberate all men, poor and rich, the oppressed and the oppressors, from all forms of oppression.

The South Korean poet, 'popular theologian' and advocate of civil rights, Kim Chi Ha, is also contributing much in the area of liberation theology. He writes:

More than anything else it was my own participation in the civil rights movement, which has been vigorously encouraged by the Korean Church since 1972, that convinced me that unrelenting resistance and the popular tradition of revolution are the materials out of which a new principle of human liberation can be forged, the principle of the unity of God and revolution. I venture to predict that this rich vein of gold, hidden in Korean earth, will bring forth a message of significance for the world, especially the Third World.[10]

'Vietnamese Catholics,' writes Nguyen Quoc Hung, 'were never in a position to develop a theology such as liberation theology. . . . Maybe the praxis of their faith will one day lead to liberation from a certain kind of theology.'[11] In his article he pleads for a constructive dialogue with socialist society.

An exception in the Asian Church scene is the Philippines, 85 per cent of whose population are Catholics. The Church is split in its opposition to the Marcos dictatorship. Persecuted Christians are growing into a suffering Church as they put their lives on the line in the defence of their own and others' human dignity and for the sake of their faith; this yields a theology addressed to the poor and persecuted.[12]

4. NEW THEOLOGICAL APPROACHES IN AFRICA

Like recent theology in Latin America and Asia, African theology, too, is trying to reflect on its own cultural and religious tradition. Here, too, Christianity is closely linked with the former colonial situation. Here, too, people were incorporated into Christendom against a background of violence and humiliation. So today the African Church and its theology are endeavouring to reconcile the Christian message with African culture. Evangelisation is understood as the communication of a message which gives meaning and value to the lives of all men, in whatever cultural setting.[13] Thus it is the human and religious experience of peoples which is the background against which Christ can be known and encountered. This is why African writers insist on having space and freedom to develop their own form of the Church and of theology: 'Allow us to wreak havoc, as it were, upon Christianity in our continent, just as you have done in Europe and America—to put it politely.'[14]

The integration of dance into the Church's life and liturgy is regarded as an important step on the way to an African Church. 'In the future, when there is an original African theology, it will perhaps be called a theology of 'inculturation', because it will have been preceded by this festive liturgy in which a living communion with the love of the Father, the Son and the Holy Spirit—the living God made flesh—is celebrated by the bodily expression of the dance.'[15]

McVeigh refers to common themes of African theology.[16] The first is the *unity* of sacred and secular, individual and community, the living and the dead. The second common element is *continuity* with the traditional African heritage, the historic Christian faith and world-wide Christianity. The 1977 Pan-African Conference of Third World Theologians, meeting in Accra, said that the sources of today's theology are an African anthropololgy, the traditional religions of Africa and the independent African churches, which are more concerned than the missionary churches to put the Christian faith forward as the answer to Africa's traditional problems. The Bible is theology's prime source, and the return to Scripture is regarded as the chief means of renewing the Church.[17]

The third common theme in African theology is that of *liberation*. Here, in contrast to Latin American theology, it is seen more as healing, wholeness and redemption. There is a confluence of three streams in this African understanding of liberation: the liberation from sin (the missionary churches), liberation from oppressive political, social and economic conditions (Latin American liberation theology) and liberation from the objective evil powers which lie behind drought, misfortune and life's daily tragedies (African tradition). African theology's contribution to liberation would be a synthesis of these three streams.

Translated by Graham Harrison

Notes

* A synopsis of 'Third World' articles in *Concilium* is available from the General Secretariat.

1. E.g., C. Jaime Snoek 'The Third World, Revolution and Christianity' in *Concilium* vol. 5 no. 2 (1966) 18-27; 'Documentation: Peace through Revolution' in *Concilium* vol. 5 no. 4 (1968) 75-87; Gustavo Perez-Ramirez 'The Church and the Social Revolution in Latin America' in *Concilium* vol. 6 no. 4 (1968) 65-70.

2. See Gustavo Gutierrez 'Liberation, Theology and Proclamation' in *Concilium* 96 (1974) 57-77.

3. See Segundo Galilea, 'Liberation as an Encounter with Politics and Contemplation' in *Concilium* 96 (1974) 19-33.

4. Enrique Dussel 'Domination—Liberation: A New Approach' in *Concilium* 96 (1974) 34-56.

5. Thus Assmann has no time for the pastoral value of popular religious practices. See Hugo Assmann 'Political Commitment in the Context of the Class Struggle' in *Concilium* 84 (1973) 93-101; Segundo Galilea (see above); *id.* 'The Theology of Liberation and the Place of "Folk Religion"' in *Concilium* 136 (1980) 40-45.

6. Jon Sobrino 'A Crucified People's Faith in the Son of God' in *Concilium* 153 (1982) 23-28.

7. Ignacio Ellacuria 'The Kingdom of God and Unemployment in the Third World' in *Concilium* 160 (1982) 91-96.

8. *Ibid.* p. 94.

9. Duraisamy Amalorpavadass 'The Poor with No Voice and No Power' in *Concilium* 146 (1981) 45-52.

10. In: Famio Tabuchi, in an article published in the other language editions of *Concilium* for 1978 but not included in the English language edition.

11. Nguyen Quoc Hung, in an article published in the other language editions of *Concilium* for 1978 but not included in the English language edition.

12. See Maria Goretti/Domingo Sale 'The Church and the Human Rights Struggle in the

Philippines' in *Concilium* 124 (1979) 92-99; Francisco Claver 'Persecution of Christians by Christians and the Unity of the Church' in *Concilium* 163 (1983) 24-28.

13. Mushete Ngindu 'The Church of Christendom in the Face of New Cultures' in *Concilium* 146 (1981) 53-61.

14. *Ibid.* p. 59.

15. Boka di Mpasi Londi 'Freedom of Bodily Expression in the African Liturgy' in *Concilium* 132 (1980) p. 63.

16. Malcolm McVeigh 'Africa: The Understanding of Religion in African Christian Theologies' in *Concilium* 136 (1980) 57-60.

17. *Ibid.* p. 59.

Yves Congar

Where Are We in the Expression of the Faith?

AFTER TWENTY years, has *Concilium* fulfilled the programme announced in its first editorial? Yes and no, or otherwise. The Council was not over. It was an experience that *Concilium*'s creators wished to prolong and to serve. It was an experience of—mutually fruitful—co-operation between pastors and theologians. It was an experience of renewal for the Church through openness to the findings of research, in exegesis for example, in liturgy and ecumenism—an openness to 'others'. Whereas before, the Church had concentrated on itself, its own ideas and resources, now it became more open to the world's demands, to dialogue with other Christians, looking at other religions. Pastors from Africa or the two Americas made contributions, which were unknown, for example, to Vatican I. Has *Concilium*'s intention to prolong and to serve all this been fulfilled? Yes. No. Otherwise. And what about tomorrow.

First, yes. Perhaps my own case is representative. My way of being a theologian is of course different from many of my colleagues. I am more a man of the past, I work in a more classical way. An illness of which there were signs in the autumn of 1935 and which took hold from April 1960 onwards, confines me more to the books and papers in my study. But *Concilium* does in fact bring me what I might be missing: ideas and news from all over the world, current problems, the voice of other schools and other churches. Now that I can no longer go out into the world, the world comes to me. This is also true for others who do not suffer from the same constraints. I know of no other periodical of such breadth of vision and documentation. The Council was a world-wide assembly. *Concilium*, in this respect, carries it on. To use a term from the psychological analysis of the conditions for becoming adult: *Concilium* honours the 'reality principle', meeting the *other*. It prolongs and serves the spirit of the Council.

No, or rather not altogether. This for several reasons. We wanted a very 'catholic' collaboration. No one was to be excluded. The only condition was that the contributions should be *constructive*. However, several names which appeared at the beginning later disappeared, for example, Ratzinger, Von Balthasar, Le Guillou. There has been a sort of parting of the ways! Let us be clear and frank. For good or ill, affairs in Holland and the Küng affair have cast their shadow over the magazine. We have hardly made any headway in Poland. The Vatican seems to have nurtured a certain mistrust. I spoke to Paul VI about it from the beginning. He, who was so open, remained reticent or even critical. All in all the situation has improved over the last few years.

The collaboration is 'catholic'. At least the Review has no guru and is not bound to a single school.

The original idea was to give those whose action determines the life of the Church 'very up-to-date information on new problems and new answers in all the theological disciplines, on a world-wide scale'. *Concilium* has done this. But the decision-makers and those who could take action seem to have profited very little from it. They could take more interest in certain sections. Apart from specialised periodicals, what magazine has dealt with burning issues of the liturgy, canon law or religious sociology in the way that *Concilium* has? Could it be that it has failed to deal with *immediate* pastoral problems which are what concern the decision-makers and those in a position to take action? Here, one of the structural principles on which *Concilium* is based proves inconvenient. The same text, without changes, has to be published in the various different editions and languages. Personally, I have always regretted the rigidity of this rule, although it has sometimes been beneficial. However the problem remains. *Concilium* informs those who want to know but has much less effect on those in power. In this respect it prolongs the Council only imperfectly.

On the other hand, it is also sometimes accused of not being theological enough, not faithful enough to biblical scholarship. We are aware of this reproach. However we wonder whether *Concilium* does not indeed reflect the situation of the theological sciences as a whole today. If, as is obvious and as Paul VI has said, an essential function of theology is to establish a link, a coming and going between the pastoral *magisterium* and the living culture of the world, *Concilium* has done a work of theology. The reproach is also rather broad. We should look at things more closely. The criticism made by some people of the sociology of religion section, that it is not purely sociological enough, is because of the presence of theological concerns.

The review has often been reproached for its title. The first editorial justified it and stated that it had no intention of seizing a monopoly. In the euphoria of the years 1963-64, it was a question of 'paying particular attention to the work of Vatican II and prolonging its work'. In what way? Of course *Concilium* did not want to be a commentary on the Council and its documents. Neither did it want to be merely an elaboration of the questions dealt with by the Council, often incompletely. But *Concilium* does follow these questions and the world's contributions. As the introduction to *Gaudium et Spes* recognises, these are characterised by swift and profound changes. Of course *Concilium* rapidly began to refer less to the Council. We believe it kept its initial promise *otherwise*. The formula 'Council, the whole Council, neither more nor less' cannot be adhered to by theological disciplines whose task is to mediate between the Church or the faith and a rapidly changing world. Many things which had hardly appeared in 1965 are important questions today for the servant of the faith. Should we mention some? Practical collapse of the philosophical bases of scholasticism, the generation gap, sexual liberation, inadequacy of repetitive solutions, feminism with its profound seriousness and 'infantile diseases', the vitality of local churches seeking autonomy, the recognition of the ecclesiality of other Christian communions and their ministries, pluralism, secularisation etc.

This is the landscape upon which the Council opened or half opened its windows and doors. Hence *Concilium's* annual general meeting discerns themes, which after free discussion and voting are assigned to the different sections. It is clear that, in these conditions, theology must, of course, be constructive, but also exercise a critical function, and if possible a prophetic function, too, towards a status quo which might be disregarding the actual state of things. Once some young Protestants invaded a church assembly very calmly carrying placards saying: 'We are the naphthalene of the world'. *Concilium* does not want to be the naphthalene of theology.

This shows which way it should go. It can consist only in being present to the future of the world and of the Church, in a continuity of profession of the apostolic faith. This is the very essence of Tradition. Perhaps I (together with my friend John Zizioulas) am the most 'traditional' of the editorial committee members. But I have changed, because each time I looked for myself, things were different from what I had been told. From the time of Pius X, under whose pontificate I was born, until the Council and after the Council, my Church has been through great changes. At the same time I do not feel that I have changed churches. Is this because I study history? I should like *Concilium* to approach questions historically. Unfortunately those who talk most about 'historicity' often study and practise history the least! History gives a sense of continuity within changes. It allows us to live in the present and to face the future with living roots, like a tree which only reaches a great height when it has deep roots. At the beginning *Concilium* was addressing men who had done theology many years before and who had to be put in touch with new research. Its present readership consists of men and women who were born into the post-Council spirit. The generation which opened the Council had grown up in a Church at rest and this is where they had their roots. If the only Church we knew was a Church in movement, a theology parcelled out in questions, a world in a state of ferment, a shattered culture, where could we stand and from what soil could we draw our sap? *Concilium* must bear witness to the presence of enduring principles as well as following changes and challenges. On the personal level, the sense of identity seems to us to be linked to the Church's life of worship, the celebration of the mysteries.

The most important task in the years to come, perhaps, will be for the Church to become more *world-wide*. This is something different from 'catholic'. This is a bit like the fact that in communion, there is the dogmatic level, real but theoretical, and the social level of actual relationships so that likewise, there is the dogmatic value of catholicity and the social experience of an actual world-wide church. Pius XII felt that the future would move from the Atlantic to the Pacific. Where is the Church, and where is the expression of the faith? *Concilium* has already made a successful effort to depart from the European monopoly. Not only the US but also Latin America, Africa and the Asian religions have been given a voice in it. Perhaps this is just a beginning. The adventure has begun. We do not know in advance how it will turn out. It can only be an organic growth, which needs time to germinate, grow, ripen. There will be inevitable setbacks. But this is the way we must go if we want to prolong and to serve the movement begun by the Council.

Translated by Dinah Livingstone

Karl Rahner

'In Season and Out of Season'

PAUL BRAND, Edward Schillebeeckx, Johann-Baptist Metz and Anton Weiler have pressed me to add a short contribution to the anniversary issue of *Concilium*. The request has added force since I belong to the original generation of *Concilium*'s founders, and this fact still gives me a certain satisfaction, even though my involvement, because of my age, has become very modest in recent years and for a number of years I have not even taken part in the annual planning meetings. But what shall I say in this anniversary issue? I am rather sceptical of appeals to the spirit of the Council which was the immediate stimulus for the founding of *Concilium*. I feel (to be honest) that too many endeavours, which may in themselves be quite legitimate, appeal to an indefinable entity known as the 'spirit' of the Council and would do better to argue their cases on their own merits. Of course, I recognise the undying credit due to John XXIII for calling what was, after all, a totally unexpected council, particularly as I believe that this Council will for ever mark the divide between the 'Pian era' of the Church and the new period in which the Church, despite all the tendencies working to delay it, is really becoming the *world* Church. But I also believe, with my late friend Burkhart Schneider, who knew Rome intimately, that many of the stories told about this pope are the latest version of the papal legend.

So what shall I say about *Concilium* itself? I naturally cannot assess the 190 issues of this international theological journal which appears in seven languages and has been through 19 volumes. Nor can I judge or evaluate the character of the individual sections. I cannot talk about the various statements and initiatives which have come from *Concilium* and have had an effect and influence far greater than that of the average theological journal. Nor, by any means, do I need to stress that some things, perhaps even not a few things, have been written in this journal which I do not applaud. That is, after all, obvious, and should neither surprise anyone or be made a ground for criticising anyone, if theology is a science in which everyone does not always automatically say the same thing, even if one sometimes gets the impression that this is the situation desired and regarded as the ideal by over-comfortable conservatives. I will even venture to say here that *Concilium* has now and then failed in the necessary respect and proper love which one owes even to one's opponents in the Church.

All this is, however, obvious, so what shall I really say in such an anniversary issue? All I can say is to repeat our basic conviction at the start of the journal and therefore hope that it may go on and go from strength to strength. I believe, as I have just mentioned, that the age of the Church as the Church of the whole world, of all the cultures and of world civilisation, has begun to exist. It has begun despite all the reactionary tendencies of today and despite all the dangers everywhere inherent in a world dominated by technical rationality. If the Church must nevertheless be the one Church of God's most radical self-offering in Jesus Christ to the whole world, there must be theological journals in this one world Church which strive to reflect and articulate this new situation of the Church, its faith and its theology. This task can certainly not be performed by *Concilium* alone. More limited regional theological journals also have a responsibility for the theology of the whole Church. Particularly if one believes that a theology of the world Church faces enormous tasks in all theological disciplines, tasks which call for an immense effort, beyond our capacities, one would heartily and selflessly hope that this task of a theology serving the preaching of the Gospel required today will also be undertaken by quite different, stronger and braver forces than *Concilium*.

At all events it is obvious that this pluralism in the theology of the world Church, which today is inevitable and should be accepted as a strength, needs an international journal to be a meeting place in which theologians from all over the world can collaborate. If in practice such an international theological journal exists in the Catholic Church only in *Concilium*, even someone who would like to see other journals of this sort, and regards them as necessary, would want to wish *Concilium* continued existence and successful development, even though no journal of this sort has the promise of immortality. For my part I believe that *Concilium* has no need to be ashamed of its past, but, on the contrary, can be grateful to God and to the men and women who have kept this journal going. My wish is that *Concilium* will live on bravely and joyfully and continue to carry out its task 'in season and out of season'.

Translated by Francis McDonagh

The *Concilium* Foundation

Concilium in Faith with the Council: 1985 and After

CONCILIUM was a product of the Council. Its *raison d'être* was described in the first issue, in 1965, in these words:

The title *Concilium* chosen for this series of books in no way aims to arrogate any definite, official claims to itself. On the contrary, the choice of this title means that the volumes will take cognizance of what the Church's pastoral authority, which was so remarkably expressed at Vatican II, has laid down as guidance for the faithful. Hence, in a special way, the volumes aim to continue the work of Vatican II. Moreover, this series of books is called *Concilium* because the apostolic work which Vatican II began, can only be brought to its full growth by theologians meeting and working together (*concilium, con-kalium, con-calare*), as a service of believers to believers and to the world episcopate. Finally, it is called *Concilium* in grateful recognition of the initiative of Pope John XXIII which has been so successfully continued by Pope Paul VI. Thus, *Concilium*, by its very name, is a constant admonition to us of the necessity of a never-ceasing dialogue.

After almost 20 years of *Concilium* the editorial directors of a number of the theological sections have remarked in this one hundred and seventieth volume that references to Vatican II have gradually become fewer, particularly since 1973. For many younger readers the Council belongs to the past. New situations and new problems appeared in the Church and the world and, in order to remain loyal to the spirit of the Council, this journal has had to concern itself with them. It may be true that in its texts the Council has today become a historical document, but on the other hand even at the time its essence was less the production of a series of texts than the collective experience of the permanent necessity for 'a constant renewal of the Church for its mission in the world'. The central event of Vatican II was the emergence of the conviction that the evangelical necessity for reform was the guiding principle of the life of the Church. This *need for reform* still exists today and is still a demand of our time. That is why, even in a changed situation, in the era after Vatican II, we propose to retain the name *Concilium*.

In June 1983 *Concilium*, in association with the University of Chicago Divinity School and the Tübingen University Institute for Ecumenical Research, held a symposium on 'The New Paradigm of Theology'. As a direct result of academic specialisation and the immense variety of theologies, there emerged, perhaps paradoxically, a general conviction that this new paradigm must be based on a God concerned with humanness and on human freedom and liberation. Against this background the 1983 annual meeting, which also took place in Tübingen, decided to establish three new sections (to make twelve instead of nine), but at the same time to spread the twelve volumes over two years.

In other words, we intend to *concentrate* our publication, and so meet the wishes of many readers: thus in future there will be *six issues a year*! At the same time, however, we want to *expand* the content and open up new areas, in three directions.

1. THIRD WORLD THEOLOGY

Although in the two decades of its existence *Concilium* has published more than 130 articles by theologians from the Third World, it has nevertheless been decided to set up a separate 'Third World Theology' section with an issue and editorial directors of its own. In doing this we wish to emphasise the polycentric character of the Church and theology and work against any tendency to centre theology in Europe and North America. We hope in this way to attain a real, rather than a merely notional, universality of theology. At the same time the 'Ecumenism' section will in future concern itself with the family of world religions as well as the family of the Christian churches.

2. FEMINIST THEOLOGY

In future there will also be a separate 'Feminist Theology' section, with female advisory members and two female directors. We realise that a separate section could have the effect of isolating feminist theology; i.e., it could be pushed into a corner and slip out of the sight and awareness of theology as a whole. Our intention is the opposite, and in the present situation concentrating the concerns of feminist theology in a separate section seems to us justified, at the very least on strategic grounds.

3. EXEGESIS AND CHURCH HISTORY

Finally we have decided to revive the former 'fundamental sections' of 'Exegesis' and 'Church History'. Since 1973 neither section has produced an independent issue, although their representatives have been active as advisers in the preparation of all the issues. 'Exegesis' and 'Church history' will now form a single section together, and produce its own issue every two years. This combination of two specialised disciplines may at first sight seem remarkable, but it is based on theological considerations. The idea is that the future issues will investigate, in relation to a specific theme, what role the theme plays in the Old and New Testaments and how its biblical presence continues to be influential, or is distorted, in the subsequent history of the Church. The process may also work in the other direction, and particular developments which have taken place in the course of Church history will be evaluated and assessed in the light of the narratives and attitudes of the Old and New Testaments. In this way both the normative significance of the Bible will be recognised and at the same time the power of Church history to inspire theology will be taken seriously. In any event the combination of exegesis and Church history may produce important results.

From 1985 about half of *Concilium*'s advisory committees will be made up of new members. Not only will younger theologians replace older colleagues, but the groups will also be made fully international and include more women than previously. The total number of people involved in *Concilium* is about 450 throughout the world.

In its twentieth year *Concilium* is striking out in new directions, keeping faith with the Council but alive to the changed conditions of our times.

The *Concilium* Foundation

Translated by Francis McDonagh

GOD IS NEW EACH MOMENT

Edward Schillebeeckx

IN CONVERSATION WITH
HUUB OOSTERHUIS & PIET HOOGEVEEN

In response to the probing questions of his colleagues, Edward Schillebeeckx provides a fascinating and comprehensible overview of his intellectual development and the concrete implications of the major themes in his work. **GOD IS NEW EACH MOMENT** permits an encounter with the flesh-and-blood Schillebeeckx—a man whose thinking is driven by his passionate concern to live a gospel Christianity that is engaged with the great social, political, and intellectual issues of the modern world. Clearly distilled are his ideas about Jesus, the Scriptures, ministry and sacraments, the future of the Church, the feminist movement, the liberation of the poor. **GOD IS NEW EACH MOMENT** explores the sources of Schillebeeckx' thought: the people, ideas, and experiences that have shaped his work.

144 pages   published in paperback

in the United States & Canada   in the United Kingdom
THE SEABURY PRESS   T. & T. Clark, Ltd.
Seabury Service Center · Somers, CT 06071

CONCILIUM

All back issues are still in print and available for sale. Orders should be sent to the publishers,

T. & T. CLARK LIMITED
36 George Street, Edinburgh EH2 2LQ, Scotland

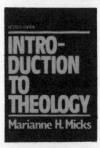